THE HITCHHIKER'S GUIDE TO THE KINGDOM

THE HITCHHIKER'S GUIDE TO THE KINGDOM

RUSSELL ROOK
with AARON WHITE

Authentic
LONDON • COLORADO SPRINGS • HYDERABAD

Equipping the Church for action

First published as Futurize in 2002 by Spring Harvest Publishing Division and Authentic Lifestyle

13 12 11 10 09 08 07 7 6 5 4 3 2 1

This edition first published 2007 by Spring Harvest Publishing Division and Authentic Media
9 Holdom Avenue, Bletchley, Milton Keynes, MK1 1QR
1820 Jet Stream Drive, Colorado Springs, CO 80921, USA
OM Authentic Media
Medchal Road, Jeedimetla Village, Secunderabad 500 055, A.P., India
www.authenticmedia.co.uk
Authentic Media is a division of Send the Light Ltd., a company limited by guarantee (registered charity no. 270162)

British Library Cataloguing in Publication Data
A catalogue record for this book is available from the British Library

ISBN 978-1-85078-734-1

Cover design by Elucid8
Print Management by Adare Carwin
Printed in Great Britain by J.H. Haynes & Co., Sparkford

DEDICATION

For Phil Wall, my original guide to the Kingdom. These few pages will never live up to all you've shown me but neither would they have been written without you. Thanks for being the best big brother I never had.

CONTENTS

	Dedication	v
	Thanks from Russell	ix
	Thanks from Aaron	xi
	Foreword	xiii
	Preface	xv
	Introduction	xvii
1	Kingdom History	1
2	Kingdom Agriculture	27
3	Kingdom Justice	53
4	Kingdom Expansion	77
5	Kingdom Economy	105
6	The Future of the Kingdom	131

THANKS FROM RUSSELL

To Charlotte, my beautiful wife, thanks for putting up with me and going the extra hundred miles every time. None of it would happen without you. To Aaron for your friendship, imagination and intellect, not to mention doing most of the work. To everyone at the Salvation Army Mission Team, thanks for writing this with me, and for me, in your prayers, testimonies, stories and dreams. To Andrea, Gill and Graeme, three of the best life-support systems that God ever made. To Adam, Andrew, Gary, Jani and Susi for calling me closer to the kingdom. To Raynes Park Community Church for being a brilliant home. To Mark Knight, a living inspiration, thanks for never letting me off the hook and for the best coffee in London. To Lesslie Newbigin, Brian Horne, Colin Gunton, Gerard Kelly, Geoff Ryan, Philip Needham, Chick Yuill, Tom Sine and the many heroes who, time and again, have turned revelation and reason into logic on fire. To the Salvation Army for wanting me, and allowing me to write, and for giving me the best job in the world. To Bob Haliday for all the support you've given and the flak you've taken on my behalf. To everyone who is part of Roots, the conference and the movement. To all my friends at Spring Harvest. To Alan, Steve, Jim and Ruth, thanks for this and all the other opportunities. To the team at Authentic, for taking a chance on me. To Ali, for more good questions than any author could shake a stick at. To Paul Yates for every sumptuous shot. To Will for digging up the details and for making footnotes fun. To all my family and my friends. Thanks for cheering me on and putting up with the long and frequent silences.

Lastly my eternal gratitude goes to the King of Kings and kingdoms. Thanks for letting me look; one day I hope to find.

Russell Rook

THANKS FROM AARON

I am afraid these acknowledgements are going to resemble the inside part of an album cover that no one reads; they will be quite boring to anyone whom I am not thanking. The thing is, you won't know if you're on the list unless you read them.

First, I must thank Russell Rook, my friend and mentor, who allowed me to participate in this book. If there is anything really thought-provoking here, it is more than likely his. If there is anything that makes no sense, or sounds really Canadian, it is almost assuredly mine.

My wife, Cherie, deserves a great deal of credit for this book, as well as for anything else I've achieved in the last several years that resembles success. I love you.

My eighteen-month-old son, Joshua, also helped in the writing process. He served as an occasional illustrative example, and also managed to reach the keyboard a few times, leaving little incomprehensible messages in the middle of the text.

Others who have inspired me throughout the writing of this book, and throughout the course of my life, are:

My parents, who have always been supportive and loving to a fault; my brothers, who know what a goof I really am; my accountability partners, Jon and Joel, who lift me up with prayer, encouragement and blue tarps; my cell church, who amaze me with their maturity and hunger to learn; the Allan family, who show great grace and humility through adversity; Chris Graves, who has incredible vision, patience and resources; Glenn and Sherrie Lavender, partly because Glenn thanked me in the liner notes of his album, but mainly because of their friendship; the mighty Will Pearson, who spent countless hours footnoting the text, which I hate doing, and for which I am ever in his debt; Southmount Citadel and Victoria Citadel, two Salvation Army Corps that contributed greatly to my spiritual development; and finally, Geoff and Sandra Ryan, Corps 614, and the

Mission Team, who are all living examples of the impact of the kingdom of God in this world.

Aaron White

FOREWORD

Russell Rook is a young Christian leader who is absolutely captivated by the kingdom... God's loving purposes for a people and a world. Be warned: if you read *The Hitchhiker's Guide to the Kingdom*, you could very well become caught up in the same contagion that has gripped his life. This book could not only change your view of the future but it could also change the direction of your life.

As you read the Introduction, you will discover where Russell caught this contagion: 'For Jesus, the kingdom is an obsession. It is his life, his ministry, his waking, his sleeping, his favourite topic, the reason for his death, and the meaning of his resurrection.' In this book, Russell is an enthusiastic guide who takes us on a very intriguing tour of God's new order, including the history, agriculture, justice, expansion, economy and the future of God's kingdom.

This book not only takes the reader on an informative tour of God's kingdom but, most importantly, it also passionately presents the panorama of the future that the Creator God has in mind for us and for his good creation. It is a 'hope above all hopes.'

Never has there been a time when the people of God more desperately needed to rediscover God's purposes for the future. There are so many competing images that vie for attention, resources and our lives — from the addictions of the global consumer culture to the obsessions of pop culture. The author urges that we 'combat the mass amnesia' of a culture 'immersed in "presentness".'

Frankly, I can't remember reading a book for a number of years that brings God's kingdom to life as forcefully as *The Hitchhiker's Guide* does. I certainly gained some new insights in reading this book and it has reignited my passion for God's kingdom. Russell reminds us in his discussion of the parables that God's new order has already broken into our midst. Therefore the work of Christians 'is to show that the kingdom of God is at hand.' We are called to be a living, breathing, celebrative foretaste of the future of God right now. Before everything else, Jesus Christ challenges us to seek first the kingdom.

This is a 'must read' book for believers who are deadly serious about their faith and really want to put first things first. I would strongly recommend that you get together with some friends or in your cell group and study this book together with a single question in mind: 'how does God want me to change my life to put his kingdom first?'

So prepare to be challenged, informed and inspired by Russell Rook's breathtaking tour of God's kingdom. Watch for the helpful guideposts on your tour including: Kingdom Sightings, Notes from Fellow Travellers, Places to Go, Places to Stay and Things to Do. It is essential that you take this tour praying 'that God's kingdom will come and God's will be done' in your life, church and in God's world. Be ready to be captivated with the contagion of God's kingdom.

Tom Sine

PREFACE

'Jesus announced the kingdom, but it was the church that came.'[1] Alfred Loisy's famous maxim can be considered a compliment or a rebuke. Either we see the church as the complicating and corrupting factor in the communication of Jesus' message, or we marvel at the church as God's chosen medium for his ultimate divine revelation. Authors have spent hundreds of years and whole rain-forests of paper taking sides in this argument. Despite the many conclusions of their writings, one single truth remains beyond dispute. The kingdom of God is the central theme of Jesus' life.

History itself tells the tale of all those who have followed after Jesus and sought to engage with this most noble and dramatic of themes. The fathers of the United States of America earnestly believed that theirs was the job of building the kingdom. Their united state was to be a landing-pad for Christ's second coming. Similarly, many prophesied that the British Empire would provide the means by which Christ's kingdom would come to the world in all its fullness. More recently, church leaders have interpreted charismatic renewal as a sign of the kingdom's coming.

The list of church leaders, political figures, historians, philosophers and philanthropists that have sought to herald the coming kingdom in their life and work is well beyond the scope of this preface or, for that matter, this book. Here we are concerned with the kingdom that Jesus 'goes on about' in his stories and sermons. In particular we are focusing on the distinctive, and sometimes difficult, stories that he tells in the 13th chapter of Matthew's gospel. These stories are the definitive travel guide to Christ's kingdom. My hope and prayer is that *The Hitchhiker's Guide* will equip and excite you for your own journey towards the kingdom. I leave you with word of your destination.

'In the Kingdom of God what is common to all is life in God. It is this life in which all contradictions characterised by hostilities are annulled.'[2]

[1] A. Loisy, *L'Evangelise and l'Eglise* (Paris: 1902), p153
[2] G. W. F. Hegel, *Early theological writings* translated by T. M. Knox (Chicago: University of Chicago Press, 1948), p278

INTRODUCTION

Before You Go

While traipsing around the damp streets of London, I found myself continually confounded by my brother-in-law's knowledge. I had long been ready to play the tour guide for this visit and was unprepared for this scenario. As another series of facts and figures spilled out to the pavement in front of me, I stood back in puzzled amazement at this foreigner's knowledge of my city. Louis was more than prepared for this trip. Louis was armed with a travel guide. Having read the book and consumed the website, Louis was now wearing the T-shirt, contacting his stock-broker regarding the acquisition of shares in the company and about to negotiate a contract to edit the next edition on London. As we wandered down streets which hadn't even made it into my A-Z, visited major attractions which had not attracted my attention in the slightest, and ate in restaurants which my taste buds had longed for since I first ate solids, I began to realise that a travel guide could be a very useful thing.

Travel guides are huge business now. Travellers have come to realise the value of knowing more about the area they are visiting than is available on a conventional map. A typical guide is written by travellers, for travellers, and is designed to give the kind of 'insider' information generally known only to well-informed locals. It serves both as a defence against the possible dangers and pitfalls of a journey, and as an aid to experiencing a fuller range of all the sights, sounds, smells and tastes that are available.

A good travel guide will inform you about the historical, political, legal, economic, demographic, cultural and environmental factors which undergird a region. It will also let you in on the best places to stay for the best price; the restaurants where you can sample authentic native cuisine; the hubs where you can interact with the local citizenry; and the wide variety of attractions and leisure activities at hand. There will be notes from fellow travellers, people who have journeyed long and far into the area and reported back on their experiences. There will be examples of the regional patois, useful words and phrases that you will need to know in order to function in a foreign locale. And usually there will be colourful stories or sightings which illustrate something of the exotic, mysterious and unique nature of the land that you are visiting. These stories are a foretaste of what may soon become the reader's own story.

The aim of a travel guide is to provide suggestions on the best way for a traveller to come to know their destination. And so it is with great pleasure, and with no little trepidation, that I have written this travel guide to the kingdom of God. While I'm not sure that I know the kingdom of God any more than I know London, I can honestly say that I love it more than any place I have ever been. The kingdom of God is beyond a doubt an exotic, mysterious, and unique destination, but it is at the same time a place I feel compelled to call 'home'.

My efforts to describe this foreign yet familiar land will, I am aware, be far from complete. Fortunately, this guide is not the only one on the market. Many giants of the Christian faith have already weighed in on the subject of the kingdom, and there are numerous examples of the use of the travel metaphor. Writers have often spoken in terms of the two cities, or the two kingdoms. The traveller starts off in the city or kingdom of the world, and ends up, all things going well, in the city or kingdom of God.

Paul, for example, speaks of the journey as a race and the kingdom as his final destination (Phil. 3:12-14). He also invokes the image of Jesus destroying all earthly dominion, authority and power as his kingdom is handed over to the Father (1 Cor. 15:24-25). This image is made vivid in the book of Revelation, as we see Satan's reign coming to an end, and the inauguration of a new heaven and new earth — specifically a new holy city of Jerusalem. St Augustine of Hippo traces the history and the attributes of the two cities right from the fall of man up to his present day, in the book *City of God*.[1] Dante, in his legendary poetic journey through the circles of hell, the mountain of purgatory, and the blissful regions of paradise, skilfully opposes the rulers of the world with the reign of the King of heaven. John Bunyan tells the story of Christian the pilgrim, as he flees the city of destruction and makes the arduous journey to the

Celestial City.[2] C. S. Lewis, borrowing Bunyan's metaphor, tells of his own pilgrimage through the world and into the kingdom of God in his book *A Pilgrim's Regress*.[3]

You may find that these classic travel guides parallel your own travels in the kingdom, or you may find that they merely illuminate other aspects you have not yet noticed. Everyone's journey, while bearing some key similarities, is also unique, and cannot be entirely explained, described or understood by someone else. Nevertheless, these mighty travellers, and many others beside, have in some measure blazed the trail for our heavenly expedition.

So we have at our disposal a wealth of travel journals from experienced kingdom pilgrims. But all of these must be considered secondary compared to the information provided by the one true kingdom 'insider'. For Jesus, the kingdom is an obsession. It is his life, his ministry, his waking and sleeping, his favourite discussion topic, the reason for his death, and the meaning of his resurrection. As Jesus describes it, the kingdom of God is the answer to a question, the significance of a story, the meaning of all miracles and the hope above all hope. It is now and not yet, here and on its way, lost and yet found, immanent and yet imminent. It can be discovered in a mustard seed, a field, or a pearl, and yet no sooner is it grasped than it slips through our fingers and merges into mystery once more. It strikes fear into theologians, leaving them to ponder the imponderable. It strikes hope into a world looking for a king and anticipation into a church longing for her royal wedding. Jesus knows the kingdom, and we would do well to listen to his stories.

Soaked in their kingdom-speak, the gospels leave us with many more definite questions than concrete answers. Christ gave us a kingdom of paradox in which to travel and explore. Is the kingdom on its way or is it already with us? Is the kingdom in the church or is it all around us? Is the kingdom changed by me or am I a simple subject? The list goes on. Through all the questioning, the king's own vision of the kingdom remains and pervades. This kingdom is about the active rule of the Creator and the loving sovereignty of the King. It is a mysterious movement for change and an irresistible instigation of eternity. It brings a futuristic plan of perfection into a very imperfect present. It scrawls eternity on our hearts and brings us heaven in the here and now. It makes us want to cry, 'Your kingdom come!'

Jesus' own travel guide to the kingdom can be found in the thirteenth chapter of Matthew's gospel. Here we discover a series of stories — more accurately called parables - which let us in on some of the divine secrets of the King of Kings. In these deceptively simple parables we come to see the world as it is, as it is meant to be and as it will be. These are not innocent little inspirational stories, moral examples, or historical allegories.[4] They are not Jesus' version of *Chicken Soup for the Christian Soul*. They are too complex, too mysterious and too testing to be considered as such. In and through these stories, God's tomorrow invades our today and brings us into his future, now.

It is no exaggeration to say that these parables turn the world upside-down. And while these stories do not contain everything that is known or can be known about the kingdom of God, they are wonderful examples not only of what Jesus had to say about the kingdom, but also of how he chose to say it. So we will explore these parables, one at a time, and in some depth. We will not rush this guided tour. We will delve into their historical nooks and crannies, tarry in their devotional rest areas, investigate their unexpected cul-de-sacs, challenge ourselves with their sudden twists and turns, and breathe in their divine atmosphere. We will not be satisfied simply by visiting them. We will try to find our home in them.

My hope and prayer is that this book can become a guide to seeking, finding and grasping the kingdom as a vision of God's ideal for creation. On a personal note, exploring these sights and sounds, these thoroughfares and alleyways, has been heavenly, and if only a glimmer of the kingdom is glimpsed in these few pages then it should be worth reading. What I do know for certain is that the kingdom is the Creator's vision for his world. It is the perfection of creation. The world as it is meant to be. The world that is becoming. In short, welcome to the real world.

Now, before you embark on this journey, please learn from my mistakes. The travel books on my shelves journeyed straight from the book shop to the suitcase. Having arrived at my destination, I usually skipped right to the big attractions and their glossy photos. On the plane home, having run out of other reading material, I finally turned to the metaphorically small print of the introductory chapters. Each section of 'things to do before you go', 'things to buy before you go' and generally 'things to know before you go' tended to strike me like lightning. 'Oh no!' I cry, 'why didn't I read this before I went?!' Take my advice: don't skip the introductory blurb, or the section on kingdom history, as you'll find that the trip is a lot less enjoyable, and maybe even more dangerous. (Now I am sounding like my brother-in-law).

A fellow traveller once warned that anyone who sets out to discover the kingdom would have to be careful not to break their necks. The eternally pure and perfect decisions and judgements of the King are infinitely out of the reach of the traveller's gaze. The divine order and rule of a perfect Father are incomparable with what we know as reality here and now. Yet, like us, Martin Luther came along for the ride. In the process he learned that the sights of the kingdom were recognised by hearing rather than seeing; faith rather than works; and the gospel rather than the law.[5] While I hope that the revelation of the Holy Spirit will enable you to see the kingdom without damaging yourself, I also warn you to beware. You, like me, may find that the kingdom is hard to spot, and that when you do catch sight of its beauty it is not anything like you imagined it to be. Further, we cannot properly give ourselves over to the exploration of the kingdom of God if we have our hearts firmly rooted in the kingdom of this world or the kingdom of our world. With this in mind, I leave you to prepare for your journey. My one piece of advice is to arm yourself with this simple maxim:

Seek first the kingdom and everything else will be added unto you (Mt. 6:33).

Place it in your hand luggage, take it everywhere you go and your journey will not fail.

Elements of the Travel Guide

This travel guide will attempt to incorporate many of the elements found in a regular guide. It is organised under six general thematic headings:

1 KINGDOM HISTORY:
Understanding the culture and history of the region

2 KINGDOM AGRICULTURE:
Examining a very unique method for sowing seeds

3 KINGDOM JUSTICE:
God's version of Operation Infinite Justice

4 KINGDOM EXPANSION:
The kingdom is growing. But who's doing it?

5 KINGDOM ECONOMY:
Wealth and happiness can be yours, for only one small payment...

6 KINGDOM FUTURE:
Where is the kingdom going? Can we go too?

The general themes will be broken down into three to six important tourist stops for each section. The tourist stops contain detailed, verse by verse explorations of Matthew's kingdom parables. They also include other elements typical of a travel guide, such as:

LOCATION: The Scripture verses we are visiting, if there is a particular passage under discussion.

PLACES TO GO

Other Scripture passages that will help your understanding of the location you are visiting.

PLACES TO STAY
Occasional devotional rest areas such as meditations, prayers, song lyrics and poems.

USEFUL WORDS AND PHRASES
The odd helpful hint on kingdom vocabulary and vernacular.

THINGS TO DO
Advice on how actively to experience aspects of the kingdom.

NOTES FROM FELLOW TRAVELLERS
Helpful and challenging journal notes from other pilgrims.

KINGDOM SIGHTINGS
Glimpses of the kingdom found in modern stories and excerpts from works of fiction.

TOUR GUIDE INFORMATION
Periodic information from wise travellers who have very specialised knowledge of the kingdom.

REMEMBER:
A travel guide may be interesting reading on its own, but it is ultimately useless to you unless you decide to travel in the area described.
Happy travelling!

NOTES FROM FELLOW TRAVELLERS

'Any good video game involves having a series of adventures, and at the end, getting a glimpse of the supernatural.'

Douglas Coupland[6]

'Some also have wished that the next way to their Father's house were here that they might be troubled no more with either Hills or Mountains to go over; but the way is the way, there's an end.'

John Bunyan[7]

PLACES TO GO

Do not worry! – Matthew 6:25-34
Watch out – the kingdom's coming! – Matthew 3

TOUR GUIDE

Malcolm Muggeridge in conversation with Aneurin Bevan commented, 'I read *Pilgrim's Progress* again the other day, and I was enormously struck by how it stands up. What a perfect image it is of human life. [Take] Christian, [how] he changes and his character develops. He is led astray and then he finds his way again, and he listens to false counsel and then comes to realise it's false. Is he going to make it? Is he going to get to the end?' Much to Bevan's dislike, Muggeridge points out that it is this powerful and miraculous dramatisation of the human story that turned *Pilgrim's Progress* into the first novel of the English language.[8]

THINGS TO DO

Who would be king?
Take a moment to write down a job description for the King of Kings. What would you like to see in a prospective applicant? What kind of skills, gifts, abilities and personality traits would you be looking for?

USEFUL WORDS AND PHRASES

Kingdom: noun – Old Testament. The phrase 'the kingdom of God' does not occur in the Old Testament but the notions of his kingly rule are pervasive. There are various dimensions to this kingship. As the Maker and Sustainer of all that exists, he is 'the great king over all the earth' (Ps. 47:2), and 'his kingdom rules over all' (Ps. 103:19); his kingly control equally encompasses past, present and future.
Kingdom: noun – New Testament. The kingdom occurs frequently in the New Testament, especially in the synoptic gospels where it is the central theme in the proclamation of Jesus.

Basileia: noun – Greek, tr. 'kingdom' has the dynamic meaning of 'rule', 'reign', 'kingship', as well as the concrete meaning of 'realm', 'territory governed by a king.'[9]

Kingdom: noun. 'What exactly is the kingdom of God? The term defies exact definition. It's pregnant with many meanings. This is its genius, this power to stimulate our imagination again and again... The kingdom of God is the common thread woven throughout the fabric of Jesus' teaching and ministry... The vocabulary of the kingdom is constantly on Jesus' lips... His words and behaviour offer the best clues to solving this riddle of the kingdom. But in the final analysis it isn't his kingdom, nor is it ours. Always and foremost Jesus points us to God's kingdom.[10]

- -

[1] St. Augustine, *The City of God* abridged and translated by J. W. C. Wand (London: Oxford University Press, 1963)

[2] J. Bunyan, *The Pilgrim's Progress* ed. N. H. Keeble (Oxford: Oxford University Press, 1998)

[3] C. S. Lewis, *The Pilgrim's Regress: an allegorical apology for Christianity, Reason and Romanticism* (London: Fount, 1998)

[4] J. D. Crossan, *The dark interval: towards a theology of story* (California: Polebridge Press, 1988) p101

[5] T. F. Torrance, *Kingdom and the Church: a study in the theology of the Reformation* (Eugene: Wipf and Stock publishers, 1996) pp22-23

[6] D. Coupland, *Life after God* (Toronto: Pocket Books, 1994)

[7] J. Bunyan, quoted in C. S. Lewis, *The Pilgrim's Regress: an allegorical apology for Christianity, Reason and Romanticism* (London: Fount, 1998)

[8] M. Muggeridge, *Muggeridge through the microphone* (London: Collins Fontana books, 1969) p93

[9] Definitions taken from *New Dictionary of Theology* (Illinois: InterVarsityPress, 1988) p367

[10] D. Kraybill, *The upsidedown kingdom* (Scottdale: Herald Press, 1978) pp20-22

CHAPTER 1

KINGDOM HISTORY

Any royalist will tell you that a nation needs her king. The king — or queen — is the symbolic figurehead of a royal nation and the source from which all political power and authority are derived and executed. Most loyal, national anthem singing citizens of the UK have some grasp of this. Imagine, if you will, that one day the entire royal family decide they've had enough; that from now on, the country can take care of itself without their tender care and guidance. This would effect a massive change, and not just in the sales of collectable plates and other assorted royal memorabilia. The constitution, the entire structure of government within the UK, would have to be altered to reflect this absence of sovereign authority. This would also be true in Commonwealth nations such as Canada and Australia, where the British monarch is still technically the head of state, much to the bewilderment of many. A royal nation without royalty is in some respects not a nation at all. At the very least it is a completely different kind of nation.

This is a concept you need to bear in mind as you travel through the parables. Both the kingdom of Israel and the kingdom described by Jesus in the parables are 'royal territories' belonging to a sovereign King. Can we really understand what that meant to the first people who heard Jesus' world-changing stories? It is true that we can never completely enter their world. We can, however, become more familiar with the historical and cultural landscape that helped give birth to the parables, and that shaped the reaction of their first audience. To do this, we must delve into the history of the kingdom.

1.1 Has the King left the building?

The history of Israel is one that holds within it a serious tension. In one corner, there is the prophetic tradition (going back to Moses) which asserts categorically that Yahweh is King and that he alone holds Israel's destiny in his hands. In the other corner is the tradition of the monarchy (going back to Saul, but most famously expressed through David and Solomon). The nation of Israel wanted a King, just like everybody else (1 Sam. 8:4-8). The prophets warned them against it and limits to the King's power were written into Scripture, but the people would have their way, and God would (seemingly reluctantly) allow it. The rest of Israel's story is then consumed with largely disobedient kings oppressing their people and contending with Yahweh over who was really in control. The actions of the Kings of Israel and Judah brought to mind the worst excesses and abuses of the treatment meted out to the enslaved Hebrews under the Pharaohs. The results for Israel were disastrous.[1]

Israel at the beginning of the first century AD is still very much a royal nation at heart. The one small snag in this is that they no longer have an earthly king, at least not one of their own. By the time we join them in the pages of Matthew's gospel, the glories of David and Solomon are a long time faded and the efforts of succeeding generations have left a lot to be desired. Since the dark days when the ruler of Babylon kidnapped the majority of the Jewish nation and forced them into slavery, the so-called 'Holy Land' has been subject to all manner of so-called 'royalty.' The milk and honey of the Promised Land has whetted the appetite of many unwanted dictators and despots, the most recent being Caesar of Rome. The nation of Israel has been forced to suffer through the desecration of their faith, the outlawing of their language and the massacre of their men. Now, more than ever, the nation yearns for the return of their king, for the end of their exile and slavery, for the resolution of ancient tensions between God and nation, and for the long-remembered promises of the King of Kings to be realised.

Israel, however, seems no closer to being restored to its royal glory. Attempts are made by philosophers and theologians to explain the centuries of apparent divine silence and inaction: 'Maybe we have been sold into slavery.' 'Perhaps God has left us for another nation', or even, 'The God of Israel has fallen asleep.' Contemplating these most unbearable possibilities, Israel seeks to wake her God with a single prayer: 'Your kingdom come!' Israel cries. 'Your will be done!' Israel hopes.

Devastation leads to desperation. By the first century, Israel is split into numerous factions, all proclaiming their own theories and pushing their own practices. In the hills and the caves lie the revolutionaries, the suicide bombers of the day, who will stop at nothing to rid their nation of Caesar's jurisdiction. Around the synagogues, the Pharisees proselytise their own brand of righteous revolution, calling for ever more liturgically legalised lifestyles. In the desert, the Essene community lives a life of strict holiness and separation from the world, in anticipation of a climatic, apocalyptic battle between God and his enemies.

The passions of these groups and others are stirred further by the presence of a self-proclaimed 'King of the Jews.' Herod Antipas polices Israel from his palace in Jerusalem. This landmark is instantly recognisable by the sculpted stone eagle perching on its highest turret. The emblem of the Roman Empire, it reveals Herod's true loyalties and reminds passers-by that he is no more the 'King of the Jews' than Caesar is the 'Father of the Nations.' It doesn't take a historian to notice that Herod is nothing more than a local thug with a crown. Under the Roman thumb, he is employed and tolerated for his ability to scare his own subjects into submission and quash uprisings with an efficiency born out of violent terror. Herod's rule keeps the radicals at bay and saves the Romans from washing their own hands too often. Is this the king the Jewish nation has been waiting for?

Given the tragic state of the 'royal' nation of Israel, the question must be asked: does Israel have anything to live for? The answer is yes. Israel has hope and prophecy and the promise of a king who is neither Caesar nor Herod. Israel has a future which does not belong to the power-crazed rulers of the day but is instead owned and secured by God himself. The promised future is a kingdom co-owned by God and Israel, the elector and the elected, the Father and the child, the Husband and his Bride. The King and the kingdom are coming together and God's future is being brought inexorably into the world's present. Israel most definitely has a reason to live.

Yet such truth seems faded and tired to an oppressed people. Having witnessed so much tyranny, Israel has begun to forget what decent kingship looks like. The rabbis continue to spin their tales about Yahweh, the King of the heavens and the earth, but even these have become tainted by the proximity of the Roman Empire and her imitation of absolute power.

The Holy Law has become little more than a holy burden, and even the most recent prophets are being forgotten in the pain of the present. As Israel labours to spot her promised King, the odds increase that she will be mistaken and that he will remain unseen. When the King arrives, Israel's false expectations may prove to be everyone's downfall.

NOTES FROM FELLOW TRAVELLERS

'Christ became our king by obedience and humility. His crown is a crown of thorns, his throne is a cross... Jesus allowed the will of his Father to be done through Pilate, Herod, mocking soldiers, and a gaping crowd that did not understand.'

Henri Nouwen[2]

'[Jesus] must have been either the prince of impostors or, what He really was, the Lord of Lords, the King of Kings, the Saviour of mankind.'

William Booth

PLACES TO GO

Jesus as Lord, Ruler and King – Psalm 22:28, 47:2,7-8, 95:1-3, 103:19, 145:10-13
Jesus as King of Israel – Isaiah 43:15, 44:6
Look – your King is coming – Zechariah 9:9

KINGDOM SIGHTINGS

In 1993 I read a news report about a "Messiah sighting" in the Crown Heights section of Brooklyn, New York. Twenty thousand Lubavitcher Hasidic Jews live in Crown Heights, and in 1993 many of them believed the Messiah was dwelling among them in the person of rabbi Menachem Mendel Schneerson.

Word of the rabbi's public appearance spread like a flash fire through the streets of Crown Heights, and Lubavitchers in their black coats and curly sideburns were soon dashing down the sidewalks toward the synagogue where the rabbi customarily prayed... They jammed by the hundreds into a main hall, elbowing each other and even climbing the pillars to create more room. The hall filled with an air of anticipation and frenzy...The rabbi was ninety-one years old. He had suffered a stroke the year before and had not been able to speak since. When the curtain finally pulled back, those who had crowded into the synagogue saw a frail old man in a long beard who could do little but wave, tilt his head, and move his eyebrows. No one in the audience seemed to mind, though. "Long live our master, our teacher, and our rabbi, king, Messiah, forever and ever!" they sang in unison, over and over, building in volume until the rabbi made a small, delphic gesture with his hand, and the curtain closed. They departed slowly, savouring the moment, in a state of ecstasy.

When I first read the news account I nearly laughed out loud. Who are these people trying to kid – a nonagenarian mute Messiah in Brooklyn? And then it struck me: I was reacting to rabbi Schneerson exactly as people in the first century had reacted to Jesus. A Messiah from Galilee? A carpenter's kid, no less?'

Philip Yancey[3]

TOUR GUIDE

Xiphilinus

The leap of imagination necessary to understand the world in which we are travelling should not be underestimated. It is virtually impossible for us to come to terms with just how desperate Israel was for her king and her kingdom to return. By the first century, there were Jews who would do just about anything to see this vision become a reality. The historian Xiphilinus records the antics of Jewish rebels only a few decades after Christ. The following scene may disturb those of a sensitive disposition but it will certainly help you to understand just how far Israel's desperation has taken her.

'Meanwhile the Jews in the region of Cyrene had put a certain Andreas at their head, and were destroying both the Romans and the Greeks. They would eat the flesh of their victims, make belts for themselves of their entrails, anoint themselves with their blood and wear their skins for clothing; many they sawed in two, from the head downwards; others they gave to wild beasts, and still others they forced to fight as gladiators. In all two hundred and twenty thousand persons perished.'[4]

THINGS TO DO

Whose King is he anyway?

Go back to the job description of a king that you wrote during the Introduction. Review what you have written and ask yourself the following questions:

→ How much of what I have written is taken from what I know God to be?

→ How much of what I have written is an extension of what I want a king to be for me?

→ How much of what I have written is about what the king would look like if he were me?

-- --

1.2 The King is a baby!

Christmas in the modern age has become a holiday, celebrating warm spirits, family gatherings, unusual generosity and unparalleled consumerism. If there is a trace of Christ still to be found in the popular understanding of Christmas, it would probably be in the form of the nativity scene. The gentle Mary, fresh from labour, immaculately robed in blue and white. The proud but generally ignored Joseph, possibly standing near some lowing cattle. Angels, shepherds, and wise men all converging on the new-born baby, lying in a manger. This inoffensive tableau is the picture most people carry in their heads of the Christmas story.

Yet there is nothing inoffensive about the arrival of Jesus in the manger. These humble beginnings betray the royal undertones of a baby born of David's line in circumstances far from the everyday. The pregnancy of a teenage virgin, the choirs of angels, and the visitors from far and near herald a new beginning, a kingdom coming into being. It is a shocking incursion of divine presence into a rebellious world, and it meets with a violent reaction from those in power. This is a pattern for the way the world will see fit to welcome its king.

In the nativity scene, the kingdom of God finds its shocking place in a fragile, mewling baby. Don't believe for a moment that 'the little Lord Jesus no crying he makes.' Any parent will tell you that a non-crying baby is not a human baby, and there is no doubt that this baby is fully human. He is fully capable of feeling the cold, the despair, the fear and the pain of the world, and fully helpless at this point to defend himself against any of the dangers which threaten him. This is why his faithful but largely unsuspecting parents quickly whisk him away from his birthplace and into the relative safety of Egypt. Fear, vulnerability, and flight to the home of Israel's historic slavery; here is our introduction to the new King of Israel, the King above all kings.

Before long, the baby from the manger will become the nation's most controversial figure. People who meet him will either love him or hate him; indifference seems to be the only unavailable option. He will scare the powerful and comfort the powerless. He will say things that burn the ears of the religious authorities, but fire the hearts, minds and spirits of the people who follow him. The kingdom-ravings of John the Baptist will form nothing more than the polite prelude to a more outrageous movement. This transition is made patently visible in John's reluctant baptism of Jesus: the warnings are over; the King is here; and the great Father makes his pleasure known.

This far-from-regal carpenter begins to construct his kingdom from the raw material of Jewish humanity, gluing together fishermen, tax collectors, prostitutes and scribes. There are other rabbis around who are doing the same thing, but they don't have Jesus' intimate understanding of the kingdom. It is, after all, his signature tune, and as he plays, more and more of Israel's children begin to dance. Living both in hope and confusion, this ordinary band begins to wonder how well Jesus knows the King and whether or not he can get them an audience. Others begin to wonder if this man might constitute a threat to all they hold dear and sacred.

KINGDOM SIGHTINGS

Lauryn Hill is a hugely popular R&B singer. Just at the time when her career was really taking off she became pregnant. She was young, unmarried, scared and aware that the pregnancy would cause scandal and inconvenience. Despite pressure to the contrary, she chose to keep the baby and gave birth to a son, whom she named Zion. Looking back on all this, she wrote a song entitled Zion, in which she relates her experiences to those of Mary, the mother of Jesus. You can listen to this wonderful song on Lauryn Hill's CD, *The Miseducation of Lauryn Hill*.[5]

NOTES FROM FELLOW TRAVELLERS

'Having a baby seems such a natural, obvious, and rather unspectacular event. But for those who are deeply aware that we are living on a planet that is being prepared for total destruction, in a time that can be sure only of the past and the present but not of the future, and in a place that is filled with pictures of death, giving life to a new human being becomes an act of resistance. Bringing into the world a little child totally dependent on the care of others and leading it gradually to maturity is true defiance of the power of death and darkness. It is saying loudly: For us life is stronger than death, love is stronger than fear, and hope is stronger than despair.'

Henri Nouwen[6]

PLACES TO STAY

'All that is gold does not glitter,
Not all those who wander are lost;
The old that is strong does not wither,
Deep roots are not reached by the frost.
From the ashes a fire shall be woken,
A light from the shadows shall spring;
Renewed shall be blade that was broken,
The crownless again shall be king.'

J. R. R. Tolkien[7]

PLACES TO GO

Prepare a way for the Lord – Isaiah 40:1-5; Matthew 3; John 1:1-18
The birth of Jesus – Luke 2:4-7
Isaiah's prophecy fulfilled – Luke 3:4-6

THINGS TO DO

The apologist Ravi Zacharias is a man used to dealing with difficult questions. On trying to conceive of the hardest question he could ever be asked, he came up with the following: 'Define God and give two examples.'[8]

While this may seem something of a brain strain at first, it occurs to me that we all answer this question on a daily basis. All of us worship two gods. We worship the true God that was, and is, and is to come. However, we also worship the god that we have fixed in our own imaginations.

Take time to pray that God will reveal the truth, goodness and beauty of the former and show us the broken reality of the latter. Pray that God will enable you to glimpse his kingdom and his kingship. Pray that your own false expectations and selfish desires will not get in the way of the kingdom coming into your life. Give God permission to reveal himself to you in new and different ways. Pray that God will grant you the insight, the openness and the courage you need to see him in all his glory.

Zion: noun – meaning 'Israel in exile.' In the six hundred years that precede the entrance of the King of the Jews, the people of God suffer unimaginable indignities. The kidnap, divide and conquer strategy of the Babylonians has decimated the Jewish nation. They fear that they have lost the two things that made them great: their God and each other. Finding themselves scattered all over the world, an identity crisis soon sets in. This scattering has become known as the *diaspora*: noun – Greek, tr. dispersion.

Living under the rule of pagan kings and far from the comforts of home and their holy sights, the Jews are forced to find new ways of faithfulness. In these contexts, getting ahead in the world was often synonymous with the worship of foreign gods. It was at this point that the synagogue came into being. From now on, they could express their worship in a new way and in a new place.

1.3 The kingdom is like a pair of bulls...

On the face of it, Jesus suits the photo-fit of Israel's messianic expectation. He is a rabbi, he works miracles, he invokes ancient prophecy and he speaks with authority. Yet appearances can prove deceiving, and this is one book that should not be judged by its cover. Something lies beneath the kingdom-talk, the miraculous signs and the prophetic visions. There is something in this man's ministry that does not conform to the wishes of his people. Where is the talk of revolt and terrorism? When will this would-be-king begin to intimidate and depose the emperor and his unruly tenant Herod? When will he stop telling stories and show us what real kingdom power is all about?

Jesus' failure to fit the mould created for him by his people should not surprise us. When we form a picture of Jesus in our heads, do we not generally imagine a handsome, Anglo-Saxon Protestant with a neatly trimmed beard and compassionate blue eyes? And how many of us ignore the hard sayings of Jesus, sticking resolutely to those that give us comfort without challenge? We often shake our heads in disbelief over the fact that first century Jews did not recognise their Messiah when he came to them. Yet we have surely earned their ridicule when we conceive of a Jesus totally divorced from his ancient Hebrew heritage. Would we even recognise our Saviour if he appeared before us?

The point is that Jesus and his kingdom cannot be contained within a box of expectations. Jesus' countrymen discovered this two thousand years ago, and we need to understand it today. The kingdom message is rooted in both the Jewish world-view and the later Christian world-view, but it is not entirely at home in either.[9] Our travels through the kingdom, therefore, need to be firmly grounded in historical and cultural reality, but also flexible enough to follow Jesus' oft-surprising lead.

The first thing to remember is that Jesus of Nazareth is a man of his time and location. The language he speaks, Aramaic, is the language of the street. The stories he tells are drawn from popular culture. His tales involve familiar heroes and villains, and use the local landscape, populace and folklore for the backdrop. Neither Jesus nor his parables appear out of place in first century Palestine.

Yet Jesus and his parables also manage to transcend their immediate environment. The uproar that the stories cause amongst the populace is certainly not bred from familiarity. The twists, the turns and the rewritten endings make people wonder if Jesus really does belong. Has he even read the script? Doesn't he know how the stories are supposed to end? The answer to both questions is, of course, yes, but Jesus is not simply telling stories. Ultimately he intends to take his audience to a thoroughly familiar yet entirely new destination.

Through these parables, Jesus is doing no less than leading the kingdom of Israel on a journey towards the kingdom of God. But he is taking them on a route that they did not expect. In Jewish apocalyptic thought, the Messiah would lead his people out of slavery and exile, complete the renewal of all creation and initiate the eternal reign of the living God in his Holy City. Jesus' parables reveal that this is exactly what his kingdom will accomplish. They also, however, reveal that Jesus has a much grander understanding of what those accomplishments are going to look like. And his methods for inaugurating the kingdom are not going to make anyone very happy.

In particular, Jesus is going to frustrate those who want the kingdom of God to be installed through acts of bloody revolution and violent vengeance. Jesus' conspiracy theories are not found in a series of terrorist's blueprints or in a plan for civil war. His kingdom comes in friendship, forgiveness and faith. It is an entirely different kind of revolution that Jesus is inaugurating. In a world that expects a fist, Jesus offers an open palm and waits for a rusty nail.

Jesus' kingdom rejects the power of the sword for the power of the word. His kingdom comes in stories. These simple tales, as we will see, are not the stuff of fable and fairytales. Their words are sharper than any double-edged sword, their themes more powerful than any party propaganda, their impact more explosive than semtex or uranium. They change the world instantly. Their power and their poignancy outlive any ruler, nation or civilisation. Nothing can stand in their wake. To hear them is to see the kingdom come and to experience God's future now. Once in the public domain, these stories will display an immediate transformational power. They will chew up popular truth and spit it out as heresy. They will displace the old dispensation and instigate a new order. Jesus doesn't need an army to accomplish his goals. In time, the very words from his mouth will bring down Israel, the Roman Empire and any other nation that would stand in the path of their magic and mystery. Jesus' kingdom comes in parables.

TOUR GUIDE

A renowned kingdom tour guide by the name of Eduard Schweizer entitled his greatest work: *Jesus, the Parable of God*. Schweizer recognised that if we are to understand the stories of God told by Jesus, we must understand the story of God told in Jesus, for they are one and the same. Jesus is the only one who could properly tell these parables, because they are centred around the fact that the kingdom of God – 'the active rule of God' – is coming to the listeners through him.[10] Thus, the story of the Prodigal Son, for instance, is both incomprehensible and untrue unless Jesus' own story is true. John Dominic Crossan picks up on this idea, suggesting that as a result of the cross, 'Jesus died as parabler and rose as Parable.'[11] In other words, he died as a storyteller and rose as the greatest story of all time. It was only in and through the cross and resurrection that Jesus' parables could be fully verified and understood. To this end, the parables are part of the cosmic story whereby the King of the world turns up in Galilee and plants the seed of an eternal kingdom in his stories and in his story.

NOTES FROM FELLOW TRAVELLERS

'Two things are generally known about Jesus of Nazareth that are beyond historical doubt. The one is that he was crucified in the first century of the Common Era. The other is that he taught in parables.'

A. J. Hultgren[12]

'Whenever Jesus speaks about his central concern, the mystery of the kingdom of God, he does so almost always more or less parabolically. Why is it that this kingdom can not be proclaimed without the language of parables or the performance of parabolic action?'

Eduard Schweizer[13]

PLACES TO GO

Jesus' kingdom expects a different mode of behaviour – Matthew 5-7
The cross is the foolishness of God – 1 Corinthians 1:20-25
Imitating Christ's humility – Philippians 2:1-11

KINGDOM SIGHTINGS

The Exodus

The story of the Exodus is the defining moment for the people of Israel. Nothing better illustrates the relationship between the king and his kingdom than the story of Israel's escape from the clutches of Pharaoh. Each year at Passover, Jewish families retell the story and celebrate the salvation and liberation of their people. By the first century this celebration had grown into a storytelling extravaganza. The family would stay up late into the night as they shared these stories of celebration and interpretation. The Passover is not the place for solemn, soporific studies. The Passover is the place for feast and fellowship and a jolly good yarn. Both comic and tragic, these highly entertaining parables journeyed from history to prophecy, from spiritual inheritance to theological understanding and from national identity to personal testimony. What it must have been like to hear such remarkable tales of God and man.[14]

THINGS TO DO

→ Robert Farrar Capon uses the term 'left-handed power' to describe the way God has chosen to act in this world.[15] God has the power to wipe out evil and make his kingdom come immediately – he showed this 'right-handed' kind of power in the Great Flood. But he has chosen to act in a different way, a non-linear, non-interventionist way, refusing to use the force he possesses, and taking the beating himself. The ultimate example of this left-handed power can be seen in the person of Jesus Christ. Jesus could have set up a kingdom of great political and military force, but chose not to. His kingdom came in parables, and in parabolic action. He took the beating on himself.

If we are to imitate Jesus, we must commit to the use of this left-handed power as well. We must be humble, forgiving, patient, and loving even to the point where we get hurt. Think about instances when you have exercised right-handed power, or relationships where you could better imitate the attitude of Jesus. Ask God for the 'power' to limit your own power and to enter into the powerlessness and suffering of others.

→ Hold your own Passover – Jesus-style. Invite friends and neighbours round for a feast. Read the stories of the Exodus and Easter. Share with one another your own stories of rescue and redemption. Let each other in on the drama, the comedy and the tragedy of your own lives. Share the stories of saints that have gone before you in poems, readings, video and song. Another way of doing this is to ask each guest to bring a CD of a favourite song which has marked an important moment in their lives. Ask the guests to tell the stories behind the songs.

→ Watch Steven Spielberg's animated recreation of the Exodus, *The Prince of Egypt*.

- -

USEFUL WORDS AND PHRASES

Haggadah: noun – Hebrew. This form of story telling had become an art form in Jewish culture. Like any nation, Israel's identity was wrapped up in her stories, which were re-told *ad infinitum*. These stories were not merely history lessons and religious instruction. They were the stuff of life itself; drama, passion, heroism, love, comedy, tragedy, justice and redemption. This art form involved more than a day in the classroom or a night at the movies. It was life in all its wild and mysterious wonder. What we have come to know as parables are one part of the art form called *haggadah*.

- -

1.4 Parables Defined

One of the most widely read and respected kingdom tour guides in history is a scholar by the name of Joachim Jeremias. Jeremias' book, *The Parables of Jesus* forms one of the greatest works on the subject of Christ's parables.[16] One of its most famous suggestions, however, has recently been disputed and disproved. Jeremias claimed that Jesus was the first rabbi to teach his disciples using parables. Developments in the field of New Testament scholarship have revealed that this is simply not the case; there is a wealth of Jewish parables that have been used as teaching tools by rabbis dating back beyond Solomon.

Over many years these stories became a religious art form in their own right, taking their place in the great Jewish traditions of wisdom and eschatology. Rabbis would use the parable and its simple formula to help the smallest minds grab hold of heaven's greatest mysteries. The technique of the parable is to understand what is unknown by comparing it to what is known. In essence, the parable is the supreme attempt of Jewish literature to imagine what God is actually like.

One rabbi has described the parable, or the *mashal*, as a 'penny candle.' He suggests that by the light of these stories, the wisdom of the law became visible to the nation's wisest forefather, Solomon.[17] It must be pointed out, however, that the parables are not the exclusive property of the intelligentsia. They are a tool that 'bridge the gap between the common people and the highly educated. By focusing on the heart and the imagination [they] reach people on all levels, from the learned to the untutored.'[18]

Jesus, like many other rabbis, uses parables to provoke new thoughts and ideas, to confront his listeners with new possibilities, and to challenge their expectations of God and his work. These stories become the building blocks out of which his followers will build a new understanding of God, the world and their own possibilities.

His parables' characters are as well-known to the audience as our favourite pantomime dame, fairytale princess or soap opera villain. The king, the shepherd, the father, the neighbour, the merchant and the Samaritan are all instantly recognisable to the listener. Their roles are tried and tested, and the audience thinks they know exactly what to expect from them. They appear as a band of travelling actors in repertory theatre, having trodden the boards in a series of long-running Jewish productions. They can perform comedy and tragedy with equal artistry. Skilled in the art of method acting, they are nothing if not true to life, and as they perform, even we modern listeners are transported into a different time and space. First century Palestine becomes our home.

However, as mentioned in the previous chapter, while the structure, setting and characters of his stories are familiar, Jesus is more than able to keep his audience guessing with a never-ending series of surprising twists and turns. If I knew nothing else about Jesus, this one talent of his would earn my respect. I am consistently disappointed and bored by movies and television shows whose endings can be accurately predicted after watching the opening credits. This is not so much a reflection on my Sherlock Holmes-like powers of deduction, as it is on the poor state of mass storytelling that exists today. This is why I get so excited about movies which actually deliver a genuine surprise at the end. For me, Jesus is the original, though far superior, M. Night Shyamalan (the writer and director of *The Sixth Sense*, *Unbreakable*, *Signs* and *The Village*). Shyamalan is celebrated, above all, for his endings. At first, his movies seem to follow the conventional Hollywood wisdom of tension, suspension and release. The recognition of plot and characters lull us into a completely false sense of security. We are now exactly where the director wants us. With one simple twist our illusions are shattered, our prophecies become bogus and our comfort is disturbed. Disoriented, we no longer know where we are, or what will happen next. Such a shock virtually guarantees that we will return to the story once more in an attempt to gather in what we obviously missed the first time around.

This is one of the keys to Jesus' success in attracting such huge crowds wherever he goes; the audience knows there will be something worth hearing, an ending they will remember. When Jesus is in town, people come to expect the unexpected. He is predictable only in his unpredictability. And for two millennia, crowds have continued to gather in colossal numbers across the world to hear his stories told over and over again. In buying this book you yourself have bought another ticket to his show. His stories remain fresh, powerful, poignant and surprising. No matter where we go we cannot escape them. The parables are relived in newspaper columns, books and movie plots. We see them echoed in everyday work, family and community life. They are ever with us and yet still they prod us in the ribs and demand that we sit up and think. These are stories that we cannot observe from a distance; within moments of their beginning we find ourselves thrown into the heat of the action, reeling with shock, moved by compassion or excited by our prospects.

The parables are not tales of human interest but of human investment. We are wrapped up in their characters and we must make good decisions if we want a happy ending.

This is why the parable becomes Jesus' chosen weapon of controversy and revolt.[19] It is in these simple stories from the city, the sea and the farm that Jesus draws the world in and then turns it on its head. John Dominic Crossan, a well-known and controversial scholar, has identified 'parable' as the polar opposite to the storytelling form that we know as 'myth'.[20] Myth helps us to understand the world, to pull contrasting and contradictory thoughts and images into some kind of reconciliation. Myth helps us to see history as part of a larger story, and through that story myth makes order out of chaos. Myths reassure us, give us stability and help us make sense of the world. It is the myth, or 'meta-narrative', that postmodern philosophy sets itself against. Myths are totalising, and they smooth over discrepancies. Postmoderns argue therefore that myths do violence to those who do not fit into the big story, or who want to retain the integrity of their own smaller cultural stories.

The function of parable, on the other extreme, is to subvert the order that myth has created. Parables turn our world upside down. Instead of trying to reconcile contrasting thoughts and images, parables deliberately set out to create contrast. Instead of avoiding or explaining away the complex and painful riddles of human existence, parables insist that we confront, consider and question. Parables shamelessly shout aloud the fact that good things happen to 'bad' people, and bad things happen to those we thought were 'good'. Parables ensure instability, charge us to change, and make nonsense of our world-view.

These are the types of stories that Jesus uses. He does not come, initially, to reassure us, but to challenge us. He does not treat us like idiots or spiritual imbeciles. He does not gloss over our difficulties and disputes with a quick chorus of *Que sera, sera*. He is not scared to declare that there are some things that we will never understand and elements of our world that are simply beyond us. And when we do think about it, this is only right. The kingdom of God cannot be contained within our world; it must do damage to the comfortable stories and theologies that we have developed. The kingdom of God takes all of our homemade theology and homespun philosophies and turns them into fairytales and bedtime stories. We become two dimensional objects being told about a three-dimensional world; understanding will not occur until our incomplete perception of the world is smashed into a million tiny pieces and our world has become his world.

NOTES FROM FELLOW TRAVELLERS

'To his fellows Jesus seemed to be saying: whatever you hope for, whatever you want, whatever you think you should have – the kingdom is not that. It always comes as a surprise.'

Robert Funk[21]

'Even the wisest angel is perpetually surprised by God.'

St John of the Cross

PLACES TO GO

If you cling to your life, you will lose it – Matthew 10:34-39

TOUR GUIDE

'Perhaps most striking about the parables of Jesus is their ways of portraying God. The parables are thoroughly theological. But they do not get involved in descriptions of God's attributes or in theoretical discussions about God. What is characteristic rather is the sense of God's intimacy and familiarity through the use of striking but common metaphors – father, king, shepherd, the owner of the vineyard, or a woman who sweeps her house.'[22]

Hultgren talks of the two types of parable. The first he calls the 'narrative' or 'once upon a time' sort of parable. These parables are full-blown stories with a cast, a plot, a beginning, middle and end. This is the land of the Good Samaritan, the sower and the sons. The second type he calls the 'similitude' or 'as if' parables. These are all together shorter. Simple comparisons, but certainly not simplistic, they last little longer than a sentence. This is the land of the mustard seed and the leaven.[23]

KINGDOM SIGHTINGS

In the days following the massacre of children in a primary school in the Scottish town of Dunblane, a Christian minister sat in his local parish church asking himself one simple question: 'How can God be in Dunblane at a time like this?' Lacking all inspiration, he turned and left the cold church and walked towards the shrine that the school had now become. On arriving at the flower-strewn gates, he spied a circle of four young men. On the sidelines, he watched as each youth produced a cigarette lighter from his pocket and illuminated the darkness of the midnight sky. Their strangely liturgical silence was broken by a nervous suggestion, 'Well, I suppose somebody should say something?'

Turning to their spectator, one of the boys called out, 'Jimmy! You'll know what to say.' His cover broken in every way, the minister stepped into the circle. Words and imagination failing him, he summoned enough courage to pray a prayer that soon dissipated beyond the bounds of fallen memory. As he finished his forgotten intercession, something sparked in the souls of this accidental congregation.

'What kind of a world is this?' one boy awoke.

'I wish I could find faith!' came another's cry.

'Where can I find God?' pleaded the third.

Confession complete, the fourth unspeaking figure turned and cast a careful eye towards the policeman standing guard over the scene of such a crime. From deep inside the lining of his coat he produced a knife and placed it on the candle-lit floor. 'I won't be needing that any more.' His covenant explicit, the others searched their own persons for unnecessary weapons and laid them at their feet.

'How can God be in Dunblane?' the minister asked; and surprise, surprise, the king answered with a story. Not with a story of superficial apologetic or happy-ever-afters but with a story of the muck and the mess of the world. A story about the real world and all that it is and all that it isn't. A story filled with difficult questions and no easy answers. Most importantly, the story of a God who doesn't side-step sickness or duck the demonic, but a God who gets his hands dirty, tells it how it is and changes the world with his stories.[24]

A good joke, while not identical to a parable in every aspect, usually does contain a twist or turn at the end, which is the source of the humour. Here is one of my favourites:

A fire and brimstone preacher was up at the pulpit, expounding and pontificating at length about the evils of the world. 'If I had twenty barrels of whisky with me right now, you know what I'd do?' he asked the congregation.

'What?' they replied in unison.

'I'd dump it right in the river!' he shouted. 'And if I had twenty cartons of cigarettes, you know what I'd do?' he asked again.

'What?' replied the congregation again.

'I'd throw them straight into the river! And if I had twenty boxes of dirty magazines, you know what I'd do?' he asked one more time.

'What?' replied the congregation, anticipating his answer.

'I'd toss 'em into that same river! And now it's time for us to sing a hymn.'

The music director got up nervously, walked to the pulpit, and said sheepishly: 'Please turn to number 420 in your songbooks, *Shall We Gather at the River*.'

THINGS TO DO

→ Try your hand at writing a parable. Remember that the key elements are familiar characters, twists and developments that turn myth on its head, and a challenging message that forces a response from the listeners. It can be a 'secular' or a 'spiritual' parable. Either way, it will help you become more at home with Jesus' favourite teaching style, and will allow you to better appreciate his ability to create and use these stories.

→ All successful sightseeing trips rely on a decent itinerary. Take some time to consider the sites that you want to see during this next stage of the journey. What are the questions that you wish to ask Jesus? What are some of the challenges that you are facing? What difficulties do you have with his kingdom? What have you already seen of this kingdom and what are the sights that you have yet to feast your eyes upon?

→ Who doesn't fit into the 'big story' of your life? Is there anyone in your family, your work, your community or your world whom you have chosen to ignore because they would make your life more complicated? Can you allow them to puncture the bubble you have created for yourself and include their story with your own?

USEFUL WORDS AND PHRASES

Parabole: noun – Greek, tr. parable. The word *parabole* is only used in the synoptic gospels. A *parabole* is a comparison, the process whereby one idea or image is placed alongside another to make a point – e.g. 'The kingdom of God is like a mustard seed.' This is not to say that the kingdom of God is a mustard seed, but simply that there is something in a mustard seed that can help us to understand the kingdom of God.

1.5 Futurizing the Kingdom

I'm sure that many of you who have been journeying with me through the history of the kingdom will be desperate at this point to ask a question or two. While a book format doesn't really allow for such interaction, we should consider one question that I am sure will have occurred to everybody by now: 'So when will the kingdom come?' I cannot promise a full answer to this question as such mystery is *slightly* beyond the realm of my knowledge or understanding. But I will address it nonetheless, as the timing of the kingdom seems to occupy a fairly prominent space in the thinking of most travellers.

One writer has pointed out, perhaps unfairly, that the subject of the kingdom attracts all kinds of 'eschatological junkies'. [25] This term refers to all those who think that God's kingdom is exclusively limited to a spectacularly dramatic event in the future which will vindicate God, judge everyone else and put everything right. An eschatological junkie is one who sees the kingdom as an instantaneous solution to the world's problems. This kingdom solution will present itself when Jesus turns up as a divine superman and replaces this broken world with a new and unbreakable model.

Now, I certainly do believe that Jesus is returning, that there will be a judgement day, and that God has a perfect future in store for his creation. But I must admit to a certain weariness when it comes to 'end times' fascination and speculation. I cannot count the number of times well-meaning people have informed me, in no uncertain terms, that given the state of the world today — with the wars in the Middle East and earthquakes and floods and locusts all over the place — the end of the world must be just around the corner. A group of Christians even went so far as to set up television cameras by the gates of Jerusalem in December 1999, hoping to record Jesus' entrance to his holy city at the turn of the new millennium. Is this really what is meant in Revelation when it says: 'Look, he is coming with the clouds, and every eye shall see him...'? That Jesus' return would be captured on home video and DVD?

These believers at the gates of Jerusalem are not dissimilar to those people in first century Palestine who were waiting for a bloody revolution, a triumphal entry, and an all-new, all-powerful king of the Jews. Both groups tend to see the kingdom as an answer to their questions and an imposition of their kind of rule and order for the universe. The problem is, in waiting for their own self-prescribed and self-projected kingdom, they run the chance of missing out on the real thing. Their eyes are so focused on the horizon they may miss what is already under their noses.

It is easy to see, however, why the eschatology junkies get hooked on their sci-fi style interpretations of the kingdom. God's perfect, sovereign and eternal rule is obviously a long way beyond anything that we have experienced in the here and now. As I write these words, the world is swallowing a bitter cocktail of shock, hurt, confusion and grief. Terrorist attacks, military actions, insurgencies, the threat of pandemic diseases and cataclysmic natural disasters around the world have been proof enough that this world is a million miles from the kingdom of God.

Such world events actually contain a significant theological question: to what extent can a perfect God be said to be in control of human history? Current affairs confirm that the kingdom of God is somehow beyond our present experience. Perfection is unimaginable to all of us for whom glaring imperfection is the order of the day. If there is a kingdom, it must surely have more to do with tomorrow than today. I must confess that in days like these, even I begin to hope that God might appear from a phone box, beat up the baddies and make it all better. I want Jesus to be like Superman, always ready to jump in and save the day with a well-aimed blast of heat vision and an inspiring comment about truth, justice and the American way. However, the journey that we are about to take and the parables we are about to hear prevent me from turning these thoughts into prayers.

When we limit the kingdom of God to the future tense, we deny its very existence. It must either be present in all times or in none at all. That means, of course, that the kingdom must exist here and now, on this earth, as broken as it is. God has established this world as an integral part of his divine order. The fact that his creatures have rejected his perfect kingdom has left the King unperturbed; his kingship will prevail.

Through his Son, God has answered the cry of a regretful people and established his new order on the earth. On the cross, Christ has been crowned King of the world and in his resurrected life he has begun to redress the balance. The world is being remade and as new creations, we experience this at first hand. Eternal life has come early and ahead of judgement day. From this day forth, the world's future can be experienced by anyone who wants it, not as a prediction but as a fulfilled promise. All the things that are beyond fallen humanity such as forgiveness, healing, wholeness, purity and eternal life have been made available by the King. Everything that man has lost can be regained. The subjects of the kingdom are caught up and irrevocably changed as God's eternity has become their reality and God's plans have become their path. To live in the kingdom is to live simultaneously in the past, present and future; to be part of the story of creation. In this sense, the subjects of the kingdom are more important than the United Nations.[26] It is they who know how the world should be and they that have grasped that vision ahead of time. It is they that know the outcome of history and the hope of the world.

Yet, the kingdom is not just in conflict with our timetable: it is in conflict with everything that we know as human beings. The kingdom, by its very nature, never quite fits into our broken world. It is there to disturb us; to point out that it wasn't meant to be this way. The kingdom can't be grasped by a human mind, but instead seeks to shape it. The kingdom can't be crammed into human history, but rather absorbs it. The kingdom is beyond humanity, beyond intellect, beyond morality, beyond politics, beyond the church, beyond yesterday, today and tomorrow. It is God's plan for all human existence, and for that matter, all animal, vegetable and mineral existence. To this end, it is not about where the kingdom fits into our world but where our world fits into the kingdom.

So when is the kingdom coming? Simple: it has come, it is coming and it will come. It is both now and not yet. It is both imminent and immanent. This world is part of the story of God's kingdom, and while the story is not complete, it is more than begun. And it is ours, both now and forever.

'It is not that someday Jesus will do this, that and the other thing, and then the kingdom will come. It is now! Christ's promise to his disciples that they will reign with him when he is king is not a promise that is waiting to be fulfilled. It has already been fulfilled with Christ's ascension into heaven. As friends of the king we are already reigning with him...'[27]

'Note, if you will, how much distance that puts between us and certain customary notions of the main subject of Scripture. It means that it is not about someplace else called heaven, nor about somebody at a distance called God. Rather, it is about *this place here*, in all its *this-ness* and *placiness*, and about the intimate and immediate Holy One who, *at no distance from us at all*, moves mysteriously to make creation true both to itself and to him. That, I take it, is the force of phrases like "the city of God" and "the kingdom of God".'

R. F. Capon[28]

NOTES FROM FELLOW TRAVELLERS

'God's covenant with man finds its reality solely, completely and finally, in the fact that God was made man, in order that as man He might do what man as such never does, what even Israel never did, appropriate God's grace and fulfil God's law. This is what God did himself as man in Jesus Christ. For that very reason in Jesus Christ the kingdom of God is at hand, as nigh as it can get while time has not yet become eternity.'

Karl Barth[29]

PLACES TO GO

The kingdom planted in us – Psalm 24.
We have already received the kingdom of God – 1 Peter 2:9

PLACES TO STAY

Listen to the lyrics from *That Day (Moment of Clarity)* by Natalie Imbruglia[30]

THINGS TO DO

'We live in an anti-historical age. Everyone, it seems, has amnesia. We are immersed in "presentness". Both past and future are drained of content. Taught by Jesus, we comprehend the past as our own story and anticipate the future as his promise, and live with sharp-edged gratitude and vivid hope.'

Eugene Peterson[31]

Write down on a piece of paper what you have 'sharp-edged gratitude' for, and what causes 'vivid hope' in you. Share these things with one person this week, in an effort to combat mass amnesia.

USEFUL WORDS AND PHRASES

Engiken: Greek phrase, tr. 'is at hand': e.g. The time is fulfilled, or God's kingdom is at hand (Mk. 1:14). Throughout the gospels, Jesus makes the claim that the kingdom of God is at hand, is near or is within our grasp. Did Jesus mean by this that the end of the universe was near, that judgement day was just around the corner? If he did, then clearly he was wrong. Could he have meant, as many of his followers expected, that Israel was about to see the overthrow of Herod, Pilate and Caesar, and the inauguration of a new early nation of Israel with God as King? Again, if he did mean that, he was mistaken.

It seems instead that all throughout his ministry, Jesus was claiming that the kingdom was in fact present *wherever he was*. As N. T. Wright points out: '[Jesus'] public ministry was itself the true inauguration of the kingdom which would shortly be established.'[32]

[1] J. Richard Middleton and Brian J. Walsh, *Truth is stranger than it used to be* (Illinois: InterVarsityPress, 1995) pp94-96

[2] Henri Nouwen, *The Genesee Diary* (London: Darton, Longman and Todd, 1995) pp184-186

[3] Philip Yancey, *The Jesus I never knew* (Grand Rapids: Zondervan, 1995) p42

[4] D. Stern, *Parables in Midrash: Narrative and exegesis in rabbinic literature* (Cambridge: Harvard University Press, 1991) p143

[5] Lauryn Hill *The Miseducation of Lauryn Hill* (Columbia, 1994)

[6] Henri Nouwen, *Seeds of hope: a Henri Nouwen reader* edited by Robert Durback (Toronto: Bantam Books, 1989) p174

[7] J. R. R. Tolkien, *The fellowship of the ring* (London: Harpers Collins, 1995) p167

[8] R. Zacharias, *Can a man live without God?* (Dallas: Word Publishing, 1994) p323

[9] N. T. Wright, *Jesus and the victory of God* (London: SPCK, 1996) pp132, 226

[10] E. Schweizer, *Jesus, the parable of God: what do we really know about Jesus?* (Edinburgh: T. & T. Clark, 1997) pp32-33

[11] J. D. Crossan, *The dark interval: towards a theology of story* (California: Polebridge Press, 1988) p103

[12] A. J. Hultgren, *The parables of Jesus: a commentary* (Grand Rapids: W. B. Eerdmans Publishing Co., 2000) p1

[13] E. Schweizer, *Jesus, the parable of God: what do we really know about Jesus?* (Edinburgh: T. & T. Clark, 1997) p23

[14] B. H. Young, *The parables, Jewish tradition and Christian interpretation* (Massachusetts: Hendrickson Publishers Inc., 1998) p212

[15] R. F. Capon, *The parables of the kingdom* (Grand Rapids: W. B. Eerdmans Publishing Co., 1985) pp15-27

[16] J. J. Jeremias, *The parables of Jesus* (London: SCM Press Ltd, 1954)

[17] D. Stern, *Parables in Midrash: Narrative and exegesis in rabbinic literature* (Cambridge: Harvard University Press, 1991) p65

[18] A. J. Hultgren, *The parables of Jesus: a commentary* (Grand Rapids: W. B. Eerdmans Publishing Co., 2000) pp7-8

[19] Cadoux and Jeremias, quoted in D. Stern, *Parables in Midrash: Narrative and exegesis in rabbinic literature* (Cambridge: Harvard University Press, 1991) p18

[20] J. D. Crossan, *The dark interval: towards a theology of story* (California: Polebridge Press, 1988) pp31-45

[21] R. Funk, foreword to J. D. Crossan, *The dark interval: towards a theology of story* (California: Polebridge Press, 1988) pxiii

[22] A. J. Hultgren, *The parables of Jesus: a commentary* (Grand Rapids: W. B. Eerdmans Publishing Co., 2000) p10

[23] A. J. Hultgren, *The parables of Jesus: a commentary* (Grand Rapids: W. B. Eerdmans Publishing Co., 2000) p3

[24] *The Hero Video* (London Bible College 1996) London Bible College is now the London School of Theology

[25] R. F. Capon, *The parables of the kingdom* (Grand Rapids: W. B. Eerdmans Publishing Co., 1985)

[26] G. E. Ladd, *The gospel of the kingdom: Scriptural studies in the kingdom of God* (Grand Rapids: W. B. Eerdmans Publishing Co., 1959) p135

[27] R. F. Capon, *The parables of the kingdom* (Grand Rapids: W. B. Eerdmans Publishing Co., 1985) pp45-46

[28] R. F. Capon, *The parables of the kingdom* (Grand Rapids: W. B. Eerdmans Publishing Co., 1985) pp15-16

[29] K. Barth, *Church dogmatics, volume 1: The doctrine of the word of God,* part 4 (Edinburgh: T. & T. Clark, 1956) p104

[30] Natalie Imbruglia, *That day (Moment of Clarity),* (White Lilies Island, RCA/BMG, 2001)

[31] E. Peterson, *Praying with Jesus* (San Francisco: Harper San Francisco, 1993)

[32] N. T. Wright, *Jesus and the victory of God* (London: SPCK, 1996) pp471-472

CHAPTER 2

KINGDOM AGRICULTURE

The Parable of the Sower – Matthew 13:1-23

Any serious traveller needs a good map. As we journey through the territory known as the kingdom of God, we will need a very good map indeed. Many experienced kingdom travellers have commented on the perilous dangers of getting lost, waylaid or misled in this land. Fortunately, Jesus' parables about the kingdom represent the best possible map and travel guide set available. If you listen carefully enough, you will be able to seek and find the kingdom in, and through, the stories. But be warned. The kingdom may not be where you would expect to find it. Parables are a peculiar kind of map: just when you think you've arrived at your destination, you'll find they lead you in a completely new and surprising direction.

Let's begin our journey by looking at a parable that maps out the agriculture of the kingdom. It may seem strange to start our exploration with a look at farming practices, but this is where Jesus begins. If it's good enough for him, then it's good enough for us.

The parable of the sower is one of the classics. It is a definitive example of Jesus' powerful parabolic teaching style. I would imagine that, for many readers, this seemingly simple story of a farmer casting his seed to the winds is one that, alongside the Prodigal Son and the Good Samaritan, springs immediately to mind whenever the word parable is mentioned. It is certainly one I vividly remember from bedtime Bible stories and bad Sunday school dramas. This makes good sense, as the parable of the sower has been given a 'star billing' in the synoptic gospels.[1] Matthew, Mark and Luke all use it to introduce Jesus' collection of kingdom parables, and all three assign to it an unusually large amount of space and interpretation.

The undoubted importance of the parable is somewhat ironic as scholars still can't seem to agree on what it originally meant.[2] Despite the familiarity most of us feel with the story, when we really try to plumb its depths we quickly find ourselves immersed in a strange and mysterious land: a place that many have visited but few have understood. Yet we, like many scholars, priests, prophets and travellers before us, have returned to take one more look at this important but elusive landmark in Jesus' life and teaching. For Matthew, the story of the sower, the seeds and the soils takes Jesus and his disciples into brand new kingdom territory.

2.1 Unfolding the Map

Anyone who has tried to read a large, wrinkled road map in unfamiliar territory from inside a moving car will know how easy it is to make crucial mistakes in navigation. If we are going to use the parables to direct us through the kingdom of God, we must first check that we are in the right town, that we have the right map, and that we aren't trying to read it upside down.

As an evangelist and a preacher, I have long used the parable of the sower as a map or study guide. Over many years, this story has helped me to navigate the joys and woes, the triumphs and the tribulations of evangelism and preaching. It has offered inspiring insights, serious strategies and eloquent excuses when things didn't work out. This parable, however, is not merely nor even primarily a 'how-to' guide for evangelism and preaching. Rather, it is a story about the kingdom, and while preaching and evangelism are a part of that kingdom, they do not by any means constitute its full grandeur.[3] To use the parable of the sower as a study guide on preaching and evangelism would be the same as using a map of America to discover New York. While you could find it on the map and get there, you would certainly not be making full use of what you had in your hands.

This incomplete reading of the parable dates back a long way. From the early church on, preaching and sowing have been synonymous.[4] For church leaders such as John Calvin the kingdom of God was intrinsically linked with the work of the church in evangelism and preaching. Through these disciplines and practices the kingdom was forcefully advancing across the world. Thus the work of the kingdom was the work of the church, and in particular the work of the preacher and the evangelist.[5] People who were not part of the kingdom could discover it in the sermons and stories they heard from the pulpit. The end result is that the parable of the sower has too often become the 'Parable of the Evangelistic Strategy' or the 'Parable of the Good Sermon.'

In reducing Jesus' parable in this way, we become guilty of diminishing his kingdom. Surely the kingdom of God is much larger and grander than our missions and meetings. The parable of the sower is ultimately about the kingdom and the soils in which we can expect to find it. It is about the identity of the sower and the kingdom work he has already done. It is about the true return from exile for the people of God and a new way of being God's people. As we wander through this parable, we must be sure to scour the surrounding landscape for all the things we have never before noticed. We must be prepared to behold the kingdom of God at work.

KINGDOM SIGHTINGS

My friend James is a musician. James often works in schools with teams of Christian artists. Their job is to develop the students' creativity while helping them to think about important life issues. In order to do this, they take the parables of Jesus and help the students to re-enact them in their own way.

James was recently working with some students on a soundtrack for the parable of the Good Samaritan. Having divided the class up, he asked them to create various sounds, rhythms and melodies for the different parts of the story. Once they had finished, James selected a student at random and gave him the job of conductor. Standing in the middle of the room, his job was simple. As he pointed to each group of his fellow students in turn, they performed their segment of the music. Through his simple gestures a miraculous score was created, with each layer of music bringing a new aspect of the story to life. In the corner the class teacher watched with amazement.

Later that day, she explained that James' chosen conductor suffered from a mild form of autism which made communication with his classmates almost impossible. Caught up in the power of the parable, this child had not only communicated with every member of the class for the first time, but had created something beautiful in and through his classmates. Here is the kingdom of God at work.

THINGS TO DO

We have seen that we tend to miss out on a lot of what this parable has to offer. What are you missing out on in your own neighbourhood? Take a prayer walk around your community. Take the time to look around properly, and note down the things you had not really seen or noticed before. In particular, look for the places where God's beauty and work are evident in your neighbourhood. Thank him for where you can see his kingdom already present where you live, and pray that his kingdom would become more and more visible to you.

2.2 Beholding the Parable

LOCATION: That same day Jesus went out of the house and sat by the lake. Such large crowds gathered around him that he got into a boat and sat in it, while all the people stood on the shore. Then he told them many things in parables, saying: 'Behold! A farmer went out to sow his seed' (Mt.13:1-3).

Before Jesus begins his story he takes a seat. Having adopted the traditional position of a Jewish teacher, his authority is noted and he begins. The exact opening of his story is missing from many modern translations. 'Behold' he says, 'the sower went out' (Mt.13:3b). Behold is one of those great words which we hardly ever use. Maybe it is too old-fashioned. Maybe it is too serious. Behold is a word with weight. Few of us would ever consider rising from our armchair and announcing to the gathered host, 'Behold! I'll make the tea', or 'Behold! I'm off to bed'. The word is too significant, too sudden and too seismic. The word is too hefty and too likely to create false expectations for those who hear it. Behold gets people's hopes up and prepares them for the unexpected. Behold is for prophets, poets, Shakespeare, bug-eyed street preachers and Charlton Heston.

Behold is also the perfect introduction to the parables of the kingdom. It means be awake, be ready, be listening and be aware. It creates a pregnant silence into which Jesus can speak. It raises the expectation that revelations are on their way. It warns earthly men that they are about to encounter the mysteries of heaven. It comes as a health warning to all those who haven't yet glimpsed the kingdom: 'If you stick around for long enough you will never be the same.' Behold the sower! Behold the kingdom! Behold the king!

KINGDOM SIGHTINGS

My wife was walking towards her car, carrying our son, looking forward to getting home and relaxing after a hard day. But the sight that met her as she came up the street made her heart sink; three people were hovering around the car, two with pamphlets, one with a heavy, black, open book, looking for all the world like they were about to break forth into some loud and obnoxious street evangelism. As soon as my wife reached the car, the man with the thick Bible began to yell. 'ARE YOU SAVED?! DO YOU KNOW JESUS?! IF YOU DON'T ACCEPT JESUS TODAY, YOU WILL GO TO HELL!' The strange thing was that he wasn't yelling at my wife, or at anyone in particular. He was just yelling into the air.

So my wife got his attention, and inquired as kindly as she could, 'Excuse me sir, but who are you talking to?'

'Anyone that will listen', came the reply, 'sometimes it only takes a word, or a phrase, to turn someone around, to get them saved.'

'But you're talking to no one. Nobody is listening. They are just trying to avoid being harassed,' explained my wife.

They tried to rationalise their evangelistic technique by citing how Paul had preached in the market place, and how, like him, they were prepared to suffer persecution.

'But there isn't even anyone here to persecute you,' my wife pointed out, 'and even if there were people here, they would be the ones who felt under attack. Look, if this is what God has specifically told you to do, then please, by all means, ignore me and keep on doing what you're doing. But I just think there's got to be a better way to get the message out.'

There is a better way. Jesus was effective because he spoke with authority, he spoke to people, and he spoke in the right places and at the right times. The crowds were excited to hear what Jesus had to say. When he said 'Behold!', people's ears pricked up. When the gentleman who accosted my wife said 'Behold!', people's ears began fleeing, along with the rest of their bodies.

The kingdom is about more than just preaching and evangelism; and it is certainly about more than just bad preaching and bad evangelism. One word of advice: if you find that you are speaking, but nobody is listening, it may be time to try out another strategy. And please, leave my wife alone.

NOTES FROM FELLOW TRAVELLERS

'Every word God speaks to us is seed. We must not treat it casually, waste any of it in uncommitted enthusiasm, or permit it to be crowded into oblivion by the words of others.'

Eugene Peterson[6]

PLACES TO GO

Never heard anything like it – John 7:45-46; Luke 19:47-48

THINGS TO DO

Consider the following questions: Do you get a sense of anticipation, of excitement, when you are about to 'behold' the word of the Lord? Or is your automatic reaction one of turning off, or tuning out? If so, why do you react as you do? Is it because of your familiarity with the story? Or because the usual presentation of God's word lacks the inspiration and authority Jesus invested it with? Finally, do people 'hang on your words' when you speak of the kingdom?

2.3 Farming Strategies

LOCATION: As he was scattering the seed, some fell along the path, and the birds came and ate it up. Some fell on rocky places, where it did not have much soil. It sprang up quickly, because the soil was shallow. But when the sun came up, the plants were scorched, and they withered because they had no root. Other seed fell among thorns, which grew up and choked the plants. Still other seed fell on good soil, where it produced a crop — a hundred, sixty or thirty times what was sown (Mt. 13:4-8).

Much attention has been given to the various sowing strategies of the farmer in Jesus' story. Discussions as to whether a first century Palestinian farmer would be so free with his seed as to scatter it on paths, rocks and thorn beds abound. While some put it down to Jesus' obvious lack of commitment to the common agricultural policy of the day, other scholars have jumped to his rescue claiming that, while obviously not a TV gardener, the Son of the Creator must have had some idea of the goings-on down on the farm. The discussions go on, but are largely irrelevant to the average modern traveller.

This parable is not an illustration from an agricultural college textbook. The purpose of any parable is to take the earthly reality of everyday life and use it to expound eternal truth. While not all Palestinians were farmers, they would all have had a far greater connection with farm life than we ever will. When I sit down to my dinner I have no idea as to the geographical journey of the food which I am eating. For many of us last night's dinner was assembled from a global farm. Meat from South America, potatoes from Idaho and fruit from Europe are all washed down with South African wine and a cup of coffee from Papua New Guinea. We are oblivious to all of this. All we need to know is how to get to the nearest supermarket.

In first century Palestine the consumer could not be more different. He has an innate interest in what happens at the local farm, how well the present crop is doing and how efficient local methods are. For Jesus' audience a bad year meant hunger and a good year meant feast. While not everyone was a farmer, everyone relied on a farmer somewhere for their daily bread. This is the genius of the parables. A story comparing the kingdom with a farm and the king with a farmer is a story with which anyone in Jesus' audience can relate. This story breaks down barriers of education, culture and class. Even more incredibly, it is able to provide a bridge between the mind of humanity and the mind of God.

The parable of the sower locates the person and power of God in the nitty-grittyness of local life, daily provision and current affairs. Of course, for most of us today a first century Palestinian farm is about as far removed from our day-to-day reality as is culturally possible. But we have to understand the purpose and technique of Jesus' teaching so that we can translate his powerful message into our modern world. We have to see that when Jesus told his parable, all of a sudden truth beyond human comprehension became as simple and immediate to his audience as a story about a farmer who sows some seed. You didn't need to be a scholar of the law in order to grasp the kingdom of God; it was good enough to understand the basics of farming.

By bringing heavenly mystery and earthly reality together in his story, Jesus is also giving us a way of understanding his remarkable presence on the earth. In the person of Jesus we find the very nature of God in an earthy casing, framed by a dirty manger, a rocking boat filled with smelly fishermen, a heavy cross caked with blood. Suddenly, we can see that the Truth beyond human comprehension is as visible as a man telling a story about a farmer who sows some seed.

TOUR GUIDE

Many discussions have taken place as to the identity of the farmer in the kingdom parables. Robert Farrar Capon[7] has suggested that the farmer must be God the Father, and that Jesus' analogy of the seed as the word indicates that he himself is the seed that God has sown throughout the world. This reading of the story is easier to understand when we consider Mark's version of events, where the farmer sows the 'word' (Mk. 4:14). However, Matthew's narration is more explicit. In his rendition of the tale it is clear that the 'word' with which Jesus identifies the seed is not the Word of God (the *logos*). Rather, it is the word, or the message, of the kingdom (Mt. 13:19). The consensus of scholarly debate seems to side with this argument, suggesting that Jesus is the farmer and the seed represents his kingdom. The second parable we will look at, the wheat and the tares, is explicit in its identification of the Son of Man as the sower.

- -

NOTES FROM FELLOW TRAVELLERS

'On the one hand, in finite terms God is beyond human comprehension, but on the other, his infinite majesty maybe captured in vivid stories of daily life.'

B. H. Young[8]

- -

THINGS TO DO

Reflect on the following passage and consider what Jesus has done and become to enable you to seek and find him and his kingdom. As a fellow traveller, consider how far God has travelled to find you:

    To the baker, Jesus says 'I am the bread of life'
    To the electrician, Jesus says 'I am the light of the world'
    To the locksmith, Jesus says 'I am the gate'

To the farmer, Jesus says 'I am the good Shepherd'
To the undertaker, Jesus says 'I am the resurrection and the life'
To the road maker, Jesus says 'I am the way'
To the philosopher, Jesus says 'I am the truth'
To the doctor, Jesus says 'I am the life'
To the wine waiter, Jesus says 'I am the vine'
Who is Jesus to you? Where can Jesus be found in the 'nitty-grittyness' of your daily life?

PLACES TO GO

An Old Testament promise of a sower and a return from exile – Isaiah 55:10-13

USEFUL WORDS AND PHRASES

Sporos: noun – Greek, tr. seed. This word will become particularly useful for us during our journey. At different points along the way we will have cause to consider its meanings and implications for our travels. In the meantime we should consider some of the common characteristics of seeds.

+ Seeds are small, and in some cases invisible.
+ Having been planted, the amount seeds can produce can be totally disproportionate to their initial size.
+ For a seed to work it has to disappear.

2.4 Sowing Wild Oats

LOCATION: Matthew 13:4-8

Regardless of your position in the great debate on first century Palestinian farming techniques and methods, you will soon notice that in this parable the sower's strategy is to leave no clump of earth, path of mud, or heap of stones unsown. The farmer sows everywhere, regardless of the chances of success. Note, too, that Jesus is emphatic that the farmer is not sowing in the present, or about to sow in the future. The farmer has been, and gone, and sown.

Anyone who is still looking to the story in a bid to justify an evangelistic strategy has already missed the most important point. As you journey through this parable, be sure to watch where you tread, for you are walking in a great field. The field is a recurring backdrop for the parables of the kingdom and in each setting it comes to represent creation as a whole. The farmer in this story has left no part of his field unsown. The kingdom of God, therefore, has been sown everywhere. There is nowhere we can travel with our revivals, crusades and campaigns that God has not gone before us. There is no spot on this earth where God has not already placed something of his kingdom. The seed may be small, buried and even invisible, or even endangered by birds, the sun, or weeds, but it is most definitely there.

Sometimes the environments in which we live and work may not look like the kind of places where a sane farmer would try to sow. Possibly even more shocking to us is the apparent negligence of the farmer after he has deposited his seed. Our modern farming methods would have us employing various other processes for the seed's protection and nurture. As responsible sowers we would water the seed, shade it from harsh winds, keep the weeds away, pour chemicals all over it to repel insects. Jesus gives a far more ancient spin to the tale. Unaware of the science of the seed and the soil beneath the ground, the sower is left to sow and then wait for harvest. The seed becomes invisible and the sower is left to raise his head to heaven and pray that God will bring a happy ending to such humble beginnings. What does this tell us about the kingdom seed?

One thing it seems to tell us is that I am in danger of writing myself out of a job. In researching this kingdom journey, I have had to unstitch many ideas which I had previously considered to be all sewn up. I have spent the last ten years working for the Salvation Army, leading missions and training young missionaries. The role of our team is wrapped up in the kingdom, with special emphasis given to the place of evangelism within the kingdom. Our job is to recruit people, train people and mobilise people to become messengers of the kingdom. If you came to one of our training events, you would be challenged to get involved in the work of the kingdom. In my better moments I would excite you with the great visions of the kingdom in Isaiah and the picture he gives of a perfected world under the reign of God the King. I would give you the good news that in Jesus' life these prophetic words have been fulfilled. In my more manipulative moments, I would maybe turn conviction to guilt and ask you to think about your responsibility to all parts of the field. I would even infer that without you, your life, and your witness, the kingdom of God might not get to its final destination. I would challenge you with film clips, newsreels, stories, stirring backing music and passionate preaching. 'The kingdom of God is counting on you!' I would shout. 'The kingdom of God is within you!' I would cry. 'Now get travelling and take it somewhere else!'

The admission, therefore, that the kingdom has already been sown everywhere is somewhat worrying. It literally strikes the fear of God into me. If God has already sown throughout the whole field of creation, then what do we do? I know it sounds selfish but I have a mortgage and countless other bills to pay. I've never had proper employment and wouldn't know the local jobcentre if it burnt down in front of me. I need a reason to get up in the morning. I have invested more than a third of my life working with a team who seem now to be almost redundant. If God doesn't need me, then what do I do with my life?

'The fear of God is the beginning of wisdom' (Prov. 1:7). It is now that I have really come to know and value this proverb. Having come to terms with my own misunderstanding and misinterpretation of the kingdom, I have begun to understand something far more precious and powerful in its presence. Far from threatening my job, the parable offers a whole new realm of possibilities for all Christians who are passionate about the kingdom and about evangelism. If the kingdom is already out there, lurking in our lives and crammed into the smallest corners of our communities, then our job becomes much easier. Instead of becoming the sole representative of God's divine and perfect order, we become messengers who point to the things that God has already done. The work of evangelists, preachers and Christians in general is to show that the kingdom of God is at hand wherever we go.

'So if the kingdom of God is everywhere', I hear you ask 'where was it when the World Trade Center fell to the ground? 'Where was it during the devastation of the Tsunami in South East Asia? Where is it in the genocidal Darfur region of the Sudan?' The answer is simple: it was in the thousands of people queuing to give blood, cheering on the emergency services and rummaging through mangled heaps of iron in the hope of finding a life. It is in the response of groups like 'Doctors Without Borders' as they provide medical help to the dying in waterlogged villages. It is in the many men and women who are working bravely in refugee camps to save one person so that the whole world might be saved. While the kingdom may have been hidden under their feet, its fruit was borne magnificently in their lives. These are glimpses of the world as it was, is and will be. They are reminders of God's kingship in the past and the present, and they are evidence of how he is shaping the future. It may be hard to see it and at times its presence may be hardly felt, but anywhere you go in time and space the kingdom is there for those who have eyes to see. There has never been, and never will be a place, person or event that is devoid of the kingdom.

KINGDOM SIGHTINGS

When the hijacked planes flew into the World Trade Center towers, the automatic reaction of most people was to flee from the buildings as quickly as possible. But for others, like the New York City Fire Fighters, it was their job to rush into the burning structures. One such firefighter was not responsible for putting out flames or trying to save lives. His job was to comfort dying souls. He was the FDNY chaplain, and as his comrades were doing their best to extract survivors from the still-standing towers, he was moving amongst the prone and nearly lifeless bodies, administering comfort, love and last rites. The last person he spoke to was a dying fireman. The man had a request to make, but could not speak above a whisper. So the chaplain leaned in and, knowing the danger involved, removed his helmet so he could hear the man's voice. As he did so, the body of another fireman fell upon him, killing him instantly. Firefighters removed his body, took it to a nearby church, and laid it on the altar, symbolising the sacrifice he had made to show the kingdom to others in their hour of need. Right to the end this man had been determined to point out that there was another way of living and another way worth knowing. Here was the kingdom in action.

NOTES FROM FELLOW TRAVELLERS

'The kingdom of God is inexorably coming into being, even apart from human efforts to bring it about or oppose it. The man's sowing is not the main thing. There is no accent at all upon his working the soil or tending to the plants as they come up. Quite the opposite. He simply sows, then waits. The focus is directed instead on the growth and fruition of the seed that was sown. The process takes place apart from human effort. So the coming of the kingdom of God can be expected as a certainty.'

A. J. Hultgren[9]

'Jesus claims for himself and the kingdom of God the whole of human life in all its manifestations.'

Dietrich Bonhoeffer[10]

PLACES TO GO

God is building his kingdom, we are asked to watch and tell – Ezekiel 37:11-14

God desires us to be watchful servants – Luke 12:35-40

THINGS TO DO

→ Keep your eyes open today for evidence of the kingdom in your life. At your work, at home, on television, in books you read, mark down all the 'known' things you can see that give you a glimpse into the 'unknown' kingdom of God.

→ Listen to the lyrics of the Delirious song: *God's Romance*.[11]

USEFUL WORDS AND PHRASES

Mashal: noun – Hebrew, tr. 1) resemblance 2) parable. Earlier we looked at the definition of parabole, or parable. The word parable has been loaned to us by the Greeks as a description for a certain type of story or comparison. The actual Hebrew word for these rabbinic stories is *mashal*. The word literally means resemblance. A *mashal* defines the unknown by using what is known. A *mashal* makes God into a farmer, his kingdom into a seed and all of his creation into a field.

The root word from which *mashal* originates is the Hebrew word for shadow. In line with this we would do well to remember that all parables and all *mashal* have their darker side. These are not just stories of sweetness and light. They are more shady than that. Like a penny candle they can light up the night with warmth and their glow. But they also cast strange shadows and remind us how dark the darkness is.[12]

2.5 Mummy, why does Jesus talk funny?

*LOCATION: 'He who has ears, let him hear.' The disci-
ples came to him and asked, 'Why do you speak to the
people in parables?' He replied, 'The knowledge of the
secrets of the kingdom of heaven has been given to you,
but not to them' (Mt. 13:9-11).*

We have already seen that parables, by their very definition, are supposed to help clarify communication. Why, then, do Jesus' parables
always seem to make understanding more difficult as well? One preacher
has remarked that the purpose of the parables was to confuse most of
the people, most of the time. Travelling through this strange foreign
land, we can certainly relate to the confusion expressed on a regular
basis by Jesus' closest followers. 'Why do you speak to the people in
parables?' they ask (Mt. 13:10; Mk. 4:12). I get the impression that, having
heard his response, they wish they'd kept quiet.

Jesus responds to the disciples, saying 'The knowledge of the secrets
of the kingdom has been given to you but not to them' (Mt. 13:11). Jesus
has very good reasons for speaking in cryptic narrative. These stories are
the weapons of controversy. They may appear to the untrained ear to be
a series of fables and fairytales but they are infinitely more dangerous
than that. These stories disturb the status quo and welcome God's rule.
For Jesus to suggest that God's kingdom is sown everywhere and not just
located in the exclusivity of chosen Israel is to tread on dangerous ground.
He has only just begun his ministry and already he has turned on his own
people. Where will it all end? He'll be attacking the temple next and
throwing out the money changers!

Have you ever had an idea that you just knew would infuriate certain
people? Have you ever hesitated before taking a course of action
because it would put a job, or possibly a friendship, at risk? Jesus was in
a similar, though far more deadly, situation. Many listeners would never
be convinced that the kingdom he described was anything but very bad
news. At the time Jesus was telling this parable, it was still far too early to
attract such controversy directly. Don't forget that the Jews already
have a king, Herod, and deliberate talk of a new kingdom will be most

unwelcome in his courts. His father sought to put this King and his king-dom to death once before and it is unlikely that his heir will be any more gracious. Jesus must make it to Jerusalem in one piece. The King must get to his city and be crowned or else he is not the King at all.

So Jesus faces a dilemma. He must use these days to instruct his disciples. It is imperative that over the next months this muddled band of followers come to some understanding of who he is. If they fail to grasp the secrets of the King and his kingdom then the whole operation will fail. However, explicit truth brings exceptional danger. Jesus must play the Pharisees and teachers of the Law at their own game. He must expound the mysteries of his divine personality to a few, while confounding the many. He must speak in a language which is intelligible to the chosen and pig-Latin to the rest. He must be both cunning and innocent.

Parables provide the perfect vocabulary for such a subversive language. Their characters and plots are known by all, yet they resist immediate interpretation. Their indirect approach makes them possible to grasp, yet impossible to pin down. Even the most unscrupulous newspaper editor will struggle to detect their scandal with any degree of certainty. The head-line; 'A farmer went out to sow!' will never sell a newspaper. Those listening to the story may have strongly suspected that they were being insulted, left out, or subverted in some way, but they would not be able to explain exactly how.

 TOUR GUIDE

In his parabolic technique Jesus is ahead of his time. Douglas Rushkoff, a renowned GenX commentator on media and culture, has coined the phrase 'Media Virus' to describe modern examples of what Jesus was doing two thousand years ago. A media virus is a subversive message delivered through the media in such a way that no one is aware they have been subverted until it is too late. So, for example, a radical political message could be delivered by one of the characters in *The Simpsons*. We wouldn't necessarily be aware that we were being exposed to the message; we would just think we were being entertained. The message would then begin reproducing itself as people talked about the episode. It sounds sinister, but it is really just a way of getting ideas which would normally be censored out into public discussion. This is what Jesus did with his parables. He used safe packages – seemingly simple and familiar stories like the sower – to deliver his powerfully disruptive messages. These kingdom messages attached themselves to the culture of the day, and were reproduced as people and communities began repeating and passing on the stories.

NOTES FROM FELLOW TRAVELLERS

'The mystery of the kingdom is a radical mystery: even when you tell people about it in so many words, it remains permanently intractable to all attempts to make sense of it.'

R. F. Capon[13]

'In the strict sense of the word, Jesus does not teach God, he narrates God. He knows that God is not, again in the strictest sense of the word, teachable. God is, however, reportable.'

Eduard Schweizer[14]

PLACES TO GO

Hearing isn't understanding – Isaiah 6:9-13

THINGS TO DO

The news that Jesus was King was dangerous and not very well received in first century Palestine. The same could be said for today. Spend some time thinking about the way you, your church, or Christians in general try to get the message of the kingdom across. Are we 'cunning as serpents, and gentle as doves'? How can we be more 'intelligent' with our evangelism? That is, how can we ensure that we are successfully communicating the gospel to the people who have been prepared by God to hear it?

Take some time in prayer, bringing before God all the people in your life who do not yet know Jesus as King. Pray for God's wisdom in knowing how to relate the message of the kingdom specifically to each of these individuals.

2.6 Secret, Sacred Language

LOCATION: 'Whoever has will be given more, and he will have an abundance. Whoever does not have, even what he has will be taken from him. This is why I speak in parables: "Though seeing, they do not see; though hearing,

> *they do not hear or understand." In them is fulfilled the prophecy of Isaiah: "You will be ever hearing but never understanding; you will be ever seeing but never perceiving. For this people's heart has become calloused; they hardly hear with their ears, and they have closed their eyes. Otherwise they might see with their eyes, hear with their ears, understand with their hearts and turn, and I would heal them"' (Mt. 13:12-15).*

While Jesus' parables are a smoke-screen for some, they also serve as a beacon for others. The light of the parables draws the earnestly seeking traveller deep into the mysteries of God. To those who have been given knowledge, more and more is given. It is easy to underestimate the challenge that this presented to Jesus' original disciples. Can we even begin to imagine what it would be like to come to terms with the fact that one of our best friends is the Messiah? Could we ever truly believe that someone we know is both God and man at the same time? Could we comprehend the talk of an oncoming death, let alone the sight of it? How would we grasp the realisation that this man is the Shepherd of Israel and the Lamb without blemish, the King of Kings and the Servant of all? 'Many prophets longed to see what you see but did not see it, and to hear what you hear but did not hear it.' Maybe at some points the disciples wished they had not seen it either.

The learning curve for the disciples is decidedly steep. Within minutes of meeting Jesus, they are running out of words to describe their experiences. Jesus is the fulfilment of all their religious instruction to date. At the same time, nothing they learned in the synagogue could have prepared them for this. Their vocabulary used up, the disciples are left to express the inexpressible. Martin Luther has declared that the parables out of necessity present a new language to express the 'new and wonderful reality' disclosed by Jesus.[15] In the parables, Jesus hands his followers a new dictionary and thesaurus for the start of a new term, a phrase book to accompany his travel guide. These stories use the language of sacred reality. It is the language of God become man, of heaven come to earth. It is the language that can make sense of Jesus' birth, life, death and resurrection. It is the language that can make sense of the history of the Jews, the state of the world and our place in God's plan.

As travellers in the kingdom of God, this is the powerful language of our inheritance. So why is it that the language of the church has often become so static, so constrictive, so predictable, so irrelevant to our world, so, well, boring? This state of affairs cannot last. As Dietrich Bonhoeffer once wrote:

'It is not for us to prophesy the day (though the day will come) when men will once more be called so to utter the word of God that the world will be changed and renewed by it. It will be a new language, perhaps quite nonreligious, but liberating and redeeming — as was Jesus' language; it will shock people and yet overcome them with its power, it will be the language of a new righteousness and truth.'[16]

KINGDOM SIGHTINGS

I made the transition from the hot, club-like main room filled with smoke, lights, video screens, dancers and upbeat praise choruses, into the smaller, quieter side room filled only with the images and sounds of people pouring out their hearts to God in prayer. My eyes fell upon a young man kneeling, alone, in the corner. I approached him, introduced myself, and inquired if he would like me to pray with him. He responded in a slow, deep voice and a thick German accent: 'Please... talk... slow... I... don't... speak... good... English.'

The young man's name was Hans; the town was Southport; and the occasion was 'Shocking.' Shocking lives up to its name. I was fortunate enough to be on the leadership team for the event last year, and what I saw was a bombardment of multi-media displays, club-style, worship music, powerful teaching, ground-shaking prayer and celebration. Hundreds of young Salvationists came to the weekend, and I am convinced that everyone left at least a little shocked at what God had done. I found that the event had given us an excellent opportunity both to experience the awesome presence of God and to come to grips more deeply with his word.

I also found that the situation with my German friend Hans was, for me, typical of the weekend. Whenever there was a challenge to pray in groups or in partners, I seemed to hook up with someone who did not share my native language. I do know how to mumble out a few phrases in German. So I was able to say to Hans that God is wonderful, and that Christianity will cost him his life, which I think made sense to him. However, my ability to tell him that the chair he was sitting on was black was less helpful.

At another point in the weekend, I spent a good hour praying with two other German young people. I didn't understand a word they said, and they did not understand me, but all three of us were speaking the language of prayer, the language of the kingdom. It was one of the most blessed times of my life.

The whole experience taught me an excellent lesson about how we communicate the gospel. Even if the people we are witnessing to speak perfect English, I have found that we in the church do not always speak their language. This is particularly true in youth ministry. Imagine the reaction your friends would have if you explained to them that they should be washed in the blood of the Lamb and sanctified by the redeeming fire of the Holy Spirit. They would, quite rightly, look at you as if you had just beamed down from Mars. The things you say may be true, and the words you use may be English, but you have still not said anything they could really understand.

Shocking uses a language, a way of communicating, that young people can understand, but which does not in any way water down the earth-shattering, sometimes hard to swallow message of Jesus. And it teaches young people that it's OK to use that kind of language to share the gospel with their friends. This is not about playing loud music and turning on the smoke machine just for the fun of it, although I must admit it is fun. It is about creatively using the tools at our disposal to get across a message that is just as relevant and urgent now as it was in Jesus' day.

THINGS TO DO

Most people have to learn at least the basics of one foreign language in school. Take this long-buried knowledge and compose a prayer to God in a language other than your native tongue. Say the prayer out loud. It may take a long time, it may be very difficult, but it will force you to consider the kingdom of God outside of the constraints of a familiar language.

2.7 The Language of Discipleship

LOCATION: 'But blessed are your eyes because they see, and your ears because they hear. For I tell you the truth, many prophets and righteous men longed to see what you see but did not see it, and to hear what you hear but did not hear it' *(Mt. 13:16-17)*.

We have seen that the secret, sacred language of the parables is required learning for the kingdom traveller. So how do we ensure that we will have ears that hear? We first have to realise that the language of the parables is an inseparable part of the language of Christian disciple-ship. Jesus did not call his disciples to a weekly linguistics lecture or a bedtime story. He called them to follow him. The impact of the parables, therefore, cannot be assessed aside from the miracles, the prayers, the conversations, the parties and all the other aspects of life on road with the Messiah. To understand a parable was to be part of the Jesus com-munity. To speak the language was to be part of the gang. Jesus was, and is, the Rosetta Stone necessary for the translation of kingdom language.

I worry a little about this, because languages are not really my strength. While my whole family has the spiritual gift of multi-cultural communica-tion, I seemed to have been left out. My relatives converse fluently and effortlessly with the nations and often get mistaken for citizens of another country. I struggle just to master English. You see, there is an important difference between my family and me, their linguistically chal-lenged offspring. They have all lived in other countries, whereas I have not. Any decent language teacher will tell you that the best way to learn a language is to spend time in the country of origin. Beyond that there seems little point in learning a language anyway. Lessons and books may well prove helpful in assisting you to order a drink, buy a train ticket, check whether your bedroom has a sea view, and locate the toilet. They will not be able to teach you the full day-to-day, incarnational implica-tions of what it means to be part of a new geography, history and cul-ture. Those of us who attempted to master a language at school will remember the endless series of pointless discussions revolving around your name, your age, the name of your favourite pet goldfish, and whether or not you would like to purchase some furniture from a pretend relative named Uncle Raoul. Very little of this will be helpful in a foreign locale.

The same obviously applies to any traveller who wishes to learn the language of discipleship, the language of the parables. If you were to visit my office you would find all manner of books on the subject of parables. If you had a few weeks to spare you could systematically read every one. Unfortunately, at the end of this time you would be no more an expert than when you first began. Studying the parables outside of Christian discipleship is as pointless as reading a travel guide without visiting the destination in question. Reading books may provide a beginners' guide to the language of Jesus and his followers, but to become fluent you must join them. If you want to understand the language of the kingdom you must first live in the kingdom. You must spend hours, days, weeks in the presence of the king. You must listen to his stories, hear him speak in whispers, obey his edicts and love his people. You must leave your house, your home, your history, and start travelling with Jesus.

To learn this language is to become mobile like the wind. To turn your back on the old and start moving towards the new. To set out for a new and undreamed of destination that lies at the edge of your world. This is radical kingdom discipleship, and without it you will always be standing outside of the parables, looking in.

PLACES TO STAY

The language of Christian discipleship can differ according to its setting. Jesus' disciples never faced the challenge of what cars they should drive, what TV shows they should watch and who they should vote for in the next election. Likewise, our brothers and sisters around the world face different challenges in their everyday attempts to follow Jesus and speak the language of discipleship today. Words such as persecution, sacrifice and mourning, which were the common vocabulary of the language of the first disciples, sound foreign to us. However, we have everything to learn about what it means to speak and live the authentic language of discipleship from our brothers then and now.

'We do not need the grace of God to stand crises, human nature and pride are sufficient, we can face the strain magnificently; but it does require the supernatural grace of God to live twenty four hours in every day as a disciple. To go through drudgery as a disciple, to live an ordinary, unobserved, ignored existence as a disciple of Jesus. It is inbred in us that we have to do exceptional things for God; but we have not. We have to be exceptional in the ordinary things, to be holy in mean streets, among mean people, and this is not learned in five minutes.'

Oswald Chambers[17]

PLACES TO GO

Some words of Jesus that were awfully difficult to swallow – John 6:53-60

THINGS TO DO

Discipleship audit: what do you consider to be the ten essential aspects of your discipleship? Knowing what you do about the King and his kingdom, what should be the ten foundational aspects of your life as his heir and subject? When you have considered this, mark yourself out of ten for each aspect of discipleship that you have chosen. What can you do to improve your scores over the next weeks and months?

2.8 Interpreting the sower

LOCATION: 'Listen then to what the parable of the sower means: When anyone hears the message about the king- dom and does not understand it, the evil one comes and snatches away what was sown in his heart. This is the seed sown along the path. The one who received the seed that fell on rocky places is the man who hears the word and at once receives it with joy. But since he has no root, he lasts only a short time. When trouble or persecution comes because of the word, he quickly falls away. The one who received the seed that fell among the thorns is the man who hears the word, but the worries of this life and the deceitfulness of wealth choke it, making it unfruitful. But the one who received the seed that fell on good soil is the man who hears the word and under- stands it. He produces a crop, yielding a hundred, sixty, or thirty times what was sown' (Mt. 13:18-23).

Jesus' disciples still have a lot to learn about the secret speech of the parables. The next months will consist of an intensive language course in the culture of the kingdom. At this stage in the story, however, while they may be more aware of the strategy behind Jesus' parables, they are none the wiser as to the meaning of the sower. Acknowledging this, Jesus begins to interpret the parable of the sower before any more questions can be asked.

Having re-read the parable as a narrative of the kingdom and not merely a motivational tool for mission, we must now re-read Jesus' own interpretation of his tale. As a child, whenever I heard a sermon on this parable, I would try to work out in my mind where I fitted in. I would check through the various scenarios and make some kind of assessment of what I was about to do with the seed of the sermon. Was I going to be excited by the message at first and then fall back tomorrow when I encountered the thorny ground of Monday at school? Would the devil snatch back my enthusiasm immediately and leave me flat out on the path? Or would the heat of the hall and length of the sermon become the rocky ground which would lull me to sleep before the end of the service? The parable became a magazine-style self-help quiz which enabled me to mark my response to this and any other given sermon.

It is easy to get caught out trying to discern what each of the four responses to the kingdom infers. For much of the church's history we have attempted to interpret this parable allegorically. If we could only find out who the seed is, what the thorns are and what the good soil means, we would be fine. Recent discussions concerning the place of parables in their historical and regional context have proved that this is an outright mistake. The parable of the sower is not a code to crack, but rather a mystery to grasp. Instead of focusing on the four responses, we should be concerned with the main question of Jesus' parable: 'Do you understand the message of the kingdom?'[18] The answer to this question determines whether or not the seed of the kingdom bears fruit in your life. Remember, understanding the kingdom comes only from spending time in the company of Jesus, being led and discipled by him. So to what extent can you say you understand the seed, the word of the kingdom? And how much kingdom fruit will be borne in and through your life?

I was once told by an evangelist that the parable of the sower only gives us the right to expect a 25 per cent success rate in our evangelism, as only one of the four sown areas actually proves fruitful. I remember being convinced by this, and wandered off feeling better about my failures. The problem is that the parable says otherwise. Matthew and Mark suggest that we might see thirty times, sixty times or even a hundred times what was sown in the first place. In farming terms, a harvest which yields a hundred times the amount sown would require that every stalk of wheat grows two heads instead of one. This is theoretically possible, but extremely rare. Yet this is the promise of Jesus, the one who knows the agriculture of the kingdom better than anyone else. It is the promise that if we follow the master farmer through the fields of his creation, we will begin to glimpse something of the perfect future God has in store. Even better, it is the promise that we will begin to see his kingdom coming to fruition in our own lives, and then growing into a bumper crop far exceeding anything we could have ever hoped for or imagined.

THINGS TO DO

Jesus is still using the parables to sow the seeds of his kingdom into the lives of his disciples, and these seeds will continue to bear great fruit. How fertile is the soil of your life? How well do you think you understand the message of the kingdom? Where are you seeing the fruit of the kingdom growing in your life?

PLACES TO STAY

'Keep speaking, dear Christ, and keep me listening. Let your word take deep root in the soil of my life and bring forth a crop of faith and love and hope, a life lived to the praise of your glory.'

Eugene Peterson[19]

PLACES TO GO

The zeal of the Israelites was not based on knowledge of the kingdom – Romans 10:1-4

KINGDOM SIGHTINGS

When it comes to learning a new language the slightest mistranslation of a word can lead to a major misunderstanding. In the days when you couldn't count on a public facility to have indoor plumbing, an English woman was planning a trip to Germany. She was registered to stay in a small guest house owned by the local schoolmaster. She was concerned as to whether the guest house contained a WC. In England, a bathroom is sometimes called a WC, meaning water closet. She wrote to the schoolmaster inquiring as to the location of the nearest WC. The schoolmaster, not fluent in English, asked a local priest if he knew the meaning of WC. Together they pondered possible meanings of the letters and concluded that it must mean 'wayside chapel' ... a bathroom never entered their minds. So the schoolmaster wrote the following reply:

Dear Madam,

I take great pleasure in informing you that the WC is located nine miles from the house. It is located in the middle of a grove of pine trees, surrounded by lovely grounds. It has a capacity of 229 people and is open on Sundays and Thursdays. As there are many people expected in the summer months, I suggest you arrive early. This is an unfortunate situation, especially if you are in the habit of going frequently. There is, however, plenty of standing room.

Actually, my daughter was married in the WC as it was there that she met her husband. It was a wonderful event. There were ten people to every seat. It was wonderful to see the expressions on their faces.

My wife sadly has been ill and unable to go recently. It has been almost a year since she went last, which pains her greatly.

You will be pleased to know that many people bring lunch and make a day of it. Others prefer to wait till the last minute and arrive just in time! I would recommend your ladyship plans to go on a Thursday as there is an organ accompaniment. The acoustics are excellent and even the most delicate sounds can be heard everywhere.

I look forward to escorting you there myself and seating you in a place where you can be seen by all.

Sincerely,

Schoolmaster.[20]

USEFUL WORDS AND PHRASES

nimshal: noun – Hebrew, tr. 'interpretation.' In the last part of our travels we came across the *mashal*, the type of Jewish rabbinical stories that we call parables. Often a *mashal* would be followed by a *nimshal*. The *nimshal* is a short interpretation or translation of the parable's meaning.

As a teaching device a *mashal* could have two contradictory outcomes. On the one hand it could help the audience to understand the meaning of the rabbi's message. On the other hand it could obscure or obstruct the understanding of what exactly the rabbi is on about. In this second case a rabbi could employ a *nimshal* to help his audience unlock the story and gain access to its meaning. Jesus' interpretation of the parable of the sower (Mt.13:18-23) is a perfect example of a nimshal.[21]

---

[1] R. F. Capon, *The parables of the kingdom* (Grand Rapids: W. B. Eerdmans Publishing Co., 1985) p62

[2] N. T. Wright, *Jesus and the victory of God* (London: SPCK, 1996) p230

[3] J. J. Jeremias, *The parables of Jesus* (London: SCM Press Ltd, 1954) p149

[4] J. J. Jeremias, *The parables of Jesus* (London: SCM Press Ltd, 1954) pp77-78

[5] T. F. Torrance, *Kingdom and the Church: a study in the theology of the Reformation* (Eugene: Wipf and Stock Publishers, 1996) pp117-118

[6] E. Peterson, *Praying with Jesus* (San Francisco: Harper San Francisco, 1993)

[7] R. F. Capon, *The parables of the kingdom* (Grand Rapids: W. B. Eerdmans Publishing Co., 1985)

[8] B. H. Young, *The parables, Jewish tradition and Christian interpretation* (Massachusetts: Hendrickson Publishers Inc., 1998) p1

[9] A. J. Hultgren, *The parables of Jesus: a commentary* (Grand Rapids: W. B. Eerdmans Publishing Co., 2000) p388

[10] D. Bonhoeffer, *Dietrich Bonhoeffer: Selected writings* (London: Fount, 1995) p161

[11] Delirious, *God's Romance*, from the album *Glo* (Arundel: Furious? Records, 2000)

[12] B. H. Young, *The parables, Jewish tradition and Christian interpretation* (Massachusetts: Hendrickson Publishers Inc., 1998) p5

[13] R. F. Capon, *The parables of the kingdom* (Grand Rapids: W. B. Eerdmans Publishing Co., 1985) p6

[14] E. Schweizer, *Jesus, the parable of God: what do we really know about Jesus?* (Edinburgh: T. & T. Clark, 1997) p28

[15] T. F. Torrance, *Kingdom and the Church: a study in the theology of the Reformation* (Eugene: Wipf and Stock Publishers, 1996) p6

[16] D. Bonhoeffer, *Dietrich Bonhoeffer: Selected writings* (London: Fount, 1995) p161

[17] Oswald Chambers, source unknown.

[18] R. H. Gundry, *Matthew: a commentary on his handbook for a mixed church under persecution* (Grand Rapids: W. B. Eerdmans Publishing Co., 1994) p260

[19] E. Peterson, *Praying with Jesus* (San Francisco: Harper San Francisco, 1993)

[20] Source unknown

[21] D. Stern, *Parables in Midrash: Narrative and exegesis in rabbinic literature* (Cambridge: Harvard University Press, 1991) p16

CHAPTER 3

KINGDOM JUSTICE

The Parable of the Weeds – Matthew 13:24-30, 36-43

'Justice' is a pretty heavy word. It tends to evoke a variety of definitions and emotional responses, largely because everyone has experienced what they would consider to be 'injustice' at some point in their lives.

One person whom I have inflicted 'injustice' upon is my younger sister Lyndall. Lyndall is one of life's remarkable people — and for her older brother to admit that — it simply must be true. She is one of the most intelligent, able, gifted, caring and compassionate people that I know. She is also blind. I mention that last because for anyone who knows Lyndall, it is one of the last adjectives on the list that precedes her name. Within hours of meeting her, people somehow forget her disability, mesmerised instead by her abilities. In recent days Lyndall has begun work with the Salvation Army Mission Team. Watching Lyndall as a colleague, as opposed to a little sister, I have once again become an eye-witness to this phenom-enon. On calling my boss to see how she had performed at an interview, I was informed that he was considering turning her down for the post for which she had applied and offering her my position instead. I was genu-inely concerned, aware as I am that she would do a much better job than I am capable of doing.

My view of Lyndall, of course, was not always so complimentary. As anyone who grew up with younger siblings will know, the sacred duty of an older brother during childhood is to keep a kid sister humble. Any tactic, no matter how dirty, is legitimate to this end. As such, I had many well-worked routines in operation to torment my sister. One of my favourites was the oft-performed miracle of water into lemonade, wherein a glass of water was surreptitiously replaced with carbonated lemonade. Now Lyndall hates all fizzy drinks, so the fun started as she tipped the glass up to her thirsty lips. Would her overdeveloped sense of smell save her? Would one of the gaseous bubbles burst on her nose, thus activating her heightened sense of touch? Or would she actually take a sip, grimace, spit lemonade all over the table and get told off for her appalling table manners? At such moments, victory was mine.

Another favourite table tactic was 'French fry fooling.' Here I would subtly remove as many of the French fries from my sister's plate as possible without her noticing. This was not as easy as it sounds. There was the immaculate timing necessary, sleight and speed of hand and, most importantly, the economy of theft. To steal too many fries would risk discovery and the administration of my mother's own swift and severe form of justice. Unfortunately, as soon as Lyndall caught a whiff of my dirty tricks, which she inevitably did, there was only one possible response. Lyndall would lift her head to the heavens and scream: 'It's not fair! He's eating my fries!' Tragically, my mother tended to agree with my sister, missing the intricate subtleties of my ego-reduction tactics.

The great themes of injustice and justice, played out around a family table. I am quite sure we all have experienced variations upon this theme. 'It's not fair!' seems to be one of the first phrases that any of us learn as children. From our earliest days, we are very concerned with the protection of our personal rights and freedoms. We want justice, at least insofar as it means getting what we feel we deserve.

We are going to be looking at a different kind of justice during our journey through the parable of the weeds. In this parable, which is also sometimes called the parable of the wheat and tares, Jesus gives us a stunning example of true kingdom justice. Injustice and oppression run rampant in our world and the issues involved tend to be terribly complex. Many hopeful do-gooders end up doing more harm than good, forgetting in their pursuit of a cause the actual humans involved. This parable, though, declares how concerned the King is with proper and careful judgement, how capable he is of administering it and how powerful his kingdom is to withstand the aggressions of would-be challengers.

3.1 That Darn Darnel

> **LOCATION**: Jesus told them another parable: 'The kingdom of heaven is like a man who sowed good seed in his field. But while everyone was sleeping, his enemy came and sowed weeds among the wheat, and went away. When the wheat sprouted and formed heads, then the weeds also appeared' (Mt. 13:24-26).

In our examination of kingdom justice, we are struck immediately by a blatant injustice. As in the first parable of the sower, here we see a farmer sowing good seed throughout his field. But this time, an enemy comes during the night and sows weeds among the wheat. The healthy, natural growth of the kingdom has been presented with an obstacle, and with a rival.

The weeds sown by the enemy were probably darnel.[1] Darnel is a poisonous weed which is closely related to wheat. Having bound itself around the roots of the wheat, it sprouts ears and becomes almost indistinguishable from the corn. The seed it produces, however, is useless. The resemblance between the wheat and the darnel is so close, and the difference between the seed so great, that darnel is commonly known as 'bastard wheat'.[2]

A rival farmer could easily plant this bastard wheat on top of the good seed, thus damaging his competitor's crop. Such agricultural vandalism could only have two outcomes. Firstly, if the weeds were confined to one small area, weeding could take place before the harvest but would cause a portion of the crop to be lost. Secondly, if the weeds were too widespread they would be left until the harvest when the wheat would be painstakingly removed from the weeds, thus prolonging the process of harvesting. In the first case, the farmer's lost wheat would push up the value of the rival farmer's crop. In the second case, the prolonged harvest would allow the rival farmer's crop to be sold first. Though repellent, these tactics were not exceptional in first century Palestine. The practice was eventually outlawed act as a crime against Roman law.[3]

Imagine the panic as the farmer's hired men awake to see weeds all around their master's wheat. Immediately the men offer to begin weeding out the darnel in order to protect the wheat. But by now it is too late; the rival has sown with a zealous and sinister enthusiasm. The weeds are not localised, but are spread throughout the field. Nothing can be done. Jesus does not talk of retaliation, but surely the men in this story would have been eager to mete out some 'field justice' of their own. But is this the will of the good farmer?

In examining this dastardly deed we are, in fact, roaming into the territory of another kingdom, one which is set in opposition to the kingdom of God. In first century Palestine, the word 'kingdom' refers to the government of the day, the one run by the political, commercial and religious institutions. But the kingdom of the world which opposes Jesus' kingdom is not solely confined to temporal authority; its source is sin, and its prince is Satan. The likes of Israel's religious caste, King Herod, and Emperor Caesar are merely bastard wheat sown to destroy the good seed of the kingdom of God. The impact of this worldly kingdom on society is both widespread and malevolent, and it infests the world with a policy of disobedience to the will of God. The fruit of this disobedience is the evil we are so familiar with in this world.

The kingdom of heaven clearly cannot stand quietly by as any rival to its sovereignty exists. It is too powerful, too promising and too pure. Still, while the first parable of the sower makes the coming of the kingdom of God the certainty of both past and present, the second parable reminds us that it is not without opposition. And the opposition would like nothing better than to infiltrate and destroy the good crop which the work of the sower is producing. So now the question is: what will the King do to save his harvest, and how will he deal with the enemy and his weeds?

TOUR GUIDE

'Satan likes to sow his tares as close to the wheat as he can, and he does sow some of them in the church. But this parable is not teaching Christians that they should tolerate unbelievers in the fellowship. We are to have nothing to do with false teachers and sham believers (2 Jn. 9-11). We are clearly commanded to purge such influences from the church (1 Cor. 5:2, 7). This parable contains instructions for the church in the world, not a free pass for the world in the church. Satan sows his people everywhere. We who belong to the kingdom exist in the same realm as unbelievers. We breathe the same air, we eat the same food, we drive the same highways, we live in the same neighbourhoods, we work at the same factories, we go to the same schools, we visit the same doctors, we shop at the same stores, we enjoy the same warm sun, and we are all rained on by the same rain. What we can never share, however, is spiritual fellowship (2 Cor. 6:14-16) and this parable does not teach otherwise.'

J. F. MacArthur Jr.[4]

NOTES FROM FELLOW TRAVELLERS

'We are planted by the Lord, in the world. We should never try to escape that. We are not told to sequester ourselves in a monastery or escape with other believers into a holy commune. We are to stay where we are planted and bear fruit. We might even have a positive effect on the tares.'

J. F. MacArthur Jr.[5]

KINGDOM SIGHTINGS

'I shall not serve.' *Paradise Lost* by John Milton is a mythical epic poem which chronicles the rebellion of Satan and the temptation and fall of humanity.[6] In the story Satan is cast as a type of tragic 'hero', crushed by a power infinitely greater than his, but still burning in hopeless, blind defiance. There is no real possibility of victory, but his strongest desire is to wage war on the kingdom of heaven, and to steal some glory from the Creator by corrupting humanity, God's greatest work. *Paradise Lost* is seen by many to be the most powerful and accurate depiction of the Prince of Darkness in literature, showing evil in all its bitterness, opposition and pathos. This is demonstrated in Satan's classic line from the poem: 'It is better to reign in Hell than to serve in Heaven.'

PLACES TO GO

One reason why we don't understand – John 8:42-47
Jesus showing the contrast of the two kingdoms – Matthew 12:22-28

THINGS TO DO

God has planted you as good seed, to bear good fruit. We know from Galatians 5:22-23 that the fruit of the Spirit is love, joy, peace, patience, kindness, goodness, faithfulness, gentleness and self-control. Take a mental inventory of your fruitfulness. Are there areas in your life where you are not exhibiting good fruit? Can you think of examples within the last few days or weeks? Are there situations coming up that you know will test your ability to bear good fruit for the Father? Pray through Galatians 5:22-23, asking God to make your life sweet and pleasing to him.

USEFUL WORDS AND PHRASES

Kingdom of heaven: gospel of Matthew
Kingdom of God: gospels of Mark and Luke

The experienced traveller will have noticed a significant difference in the guide written by Matthew and those by his contemporaries Mark and Luke. Where Matthew translates Jesus' talk of the kingdom as the 'kingdom of heaven', his colleagues prefer the phrase the 'kingdom of God.' Are there two different kingdoms of God for travellers to consider? The answer is no. The difference in wording highlights the different markets for which the authors were writing. Matthew is concerned with a Jewish audience who are conversant with the concept of 'heaven' (in first century Israel, 'heaven' was a massive discussion point in the national debate). Mark and Luke, on the other hand, are writing for a wider, less Jewish, market. Not wishing to alienate these new markets with foreign theological concepts they prefer to use the more universal word, 'God'.

3.2 A Tale of Two Cities – The Battle Royal

LOCATION: The owner's servants came to him and said, 'Sir, didn't you sow good seed in your field? Where then did the weeds come from?' 'An enemy did this', he replied...

Then he [Jesus] left the crowd and went into the house. His disciples came to him and said, 'Explain to us the parable of the weeds in the field.' He answered, 'The one who sowed the good seed is the Son of Man. The field is the world, and the good seed stands for the sons of the kingdom. The weeds are the sons of the evil one, and the enemy who sows them is the devil. The harvest is the end of the age, and the harvesters are angels' (Mt. 13:27-28a, 36-39).

You need to be constantly aware, as you travel in this land of parables, that while it is a kingdom of peace, it is also a kingdom at war. It is not the only kingdom in business, and as we have seen, God has rivals to his claim of absolute sovereignty.

This rivalry is very evident in the life of Christ. Jesus was born during the reign of Caesar Augustus, the most powerful man in the world. Augustus' kingdom was enormous, and he was able to enforce a strict peace, the *Pax Romana*, within its borders. In many ways, Augustus was the best the world could offer as far as power and glory were concerned, and it would be difficult to find another ruler in history who has wielded an equivalent amount of authority. Against this imposing figure we see the familiar setting of the nativity: a poor couple far from home, a young woman giving birth in a room occupied by animals, a hurried flight away from danger into another land. It does not seem very impressive at all. And yet the nativity is very much about the competition between two rival kingdoms, one represented (on the surface) by Caesar, the other by a little baby named Jesus: the kingdom of the world versus the kingdom of heaven.

The parable we are looking at here also illustrates this war, insofar as it contains a number of opposites. We see the good farmer pitted against his nefarious enemy, and the fruitful wheat intertwined with the poison-ous weeds. It is always tempting to see our human conflicts in the same vein. As I write this chapter, the world is still very much embroiled in the 'War on Terror' and no end is in sight. Every side in this conflict has cast things in very 'black and white' terms: good versus evil, light versus dark, the powers of freedom versus the powers of terror, imperialism versus independence, the forces of Allah versus the Great Satan. At least two of the forces involved have also claimed to have the full support of a major deity. Many Christians I have spoken with have decided that this is the battle that heralds the last times. I'm not so sure.

What we can say for sure is that the parable of the wheat and weeds, though it talks about an enemy, is not referring specifically to Caesar Augustus, nor even to Osama bin Laden. Many in Israel at the time of Jesus are trying to cast Rome as the last of the four great empires, the Satan-figure against which they had to wage holy war. In the parable of the wheat and weeds, however, Jesus subverts this traditional Jewish apocalyptic thinking. He agrees that there is an enemy to be defeated, but he locates that enemy, and the method for God's ultimate victory, in places people didn't expect. The real enemy is not an outside Gentile power. The Gentiles, too, are being held in bondage by the true enemies to God's kingdom — Satan and sin.

Against the kingdom of Satan, Israel's God is waging an effective war. But this war is not being won through overt military action, but rather through the actions and words of Jesus.[7] Paul picks up on Jesus' identification of the real enemy when he asserts that our fight 'is not against flesh and blood, but against the rulers, against the authorities, against the powers of this dark world and against the spiritual forces of evil in the heavenly realms' (Eph. 6:12). Amazing as it sounds, Paul had never even heard of Osama bin Laden.

Therefore, it is inappropriate for us to point to world leaders or terrorists as the sources of the great evil in the world; they are only 'sons of the evil one'. To be sure, terrorist acts and the evils of war and militarism stem from the influence of the kingdom of this world. But the real evil lies much deeper. If the kingdom of God is about the rule or the sovereignty of God, then the opposition is all about rebelling and trying to usurp that rightful rule. It is civil war on a cosmic, spiritual scale.

The first humans, by their own free will, chose to throw their lot in with the wrong side, and many continue to do so today. Why would anyone in their right mind join the fight against the God of creation? One reason is that the kingdom of the world deals in obvious power, in worldly strength. Temporary world peace is brought about in the first century by the threat of Roman legions, in the twenty-first century by the threat of mutual assured destruction. We humans are attracted to the display of temporal power, temporal wealth, and temporal wisdom. We can see, hear and feel what Augustus and others have to offer, and the immediate success and glory looks pretty good to our eyes.

Contrast this to the power demonstrated by God through Jesus. The one thing virtually everyone knows about Jesus is that he was killed, beaten and hung up to dry by representatives of the kingdom of the world. This is not a very attractive display of power, and our rational intellect tells us to have nothing to do with it. After all, Jesus tells his disciples that they should expect more of the same treatment from the world, doesn't he? 'All men will hate you because of me' (Mt. 10:22). There is no earthly glory to be had here. And yet, at the back of our minds we remember the claim that Jesus made: not to have brought about a temporary world peace, but rather an eternal peace between humanity and its Creator. Could it be true?

Jesus sets his kingdom up as the dangerous, radical, revolutionary alternative to the dark powers and authorities of this world. The parable of the weeds therefore forces the kingdom traveller to answer the following questions: to which kingdom do you belong? To whom will you pledge your allegiance? Will you be good seed, a true disciple, a child of the kingdom? Will you join your prayers and your life to the cause of seeing this alternative kingdom become a reality here on earth? Or will you be darnel, bastard seed, a son of the enemy, enlisted in the cause of the world and actively resisting the onset of the rule of God? Your answers will greatly impact your fate, come harvest time.

NOTES FROM FELLOW TRAVELLERS

'Who are we? The short answer Jesus might have given to the question of identity is: we are Israel, the chosen people of the Creator God. More specifically, we are the real, the true, Israel, in the process of being redeemed at last by this God, over against the spurious claimants who are either in power or mounting alternative programmes.'

N. T. Wright[8]

KINGDOM SIGHTINGS

+ The devil has logged a lot of screen time in Hollywood. I suppose he has always intrigued humanity; the writer of *The Exorcist* once said that he didn't believe in God, but he did believe in Satan, because he advertised a lot more. The devil is also a meaty character for actors to dig into, much more fun than playing a good guy, and he lends himself well to blockbuster-style special effects. But the Prince of Darkness often comes off on screen as completely unbelievable.
+ One surprisingly nuanced portrayal of Satan can be found in the movie *The Devil's Advocate*, starring Keanu Reeves and Al Pacino.[9] (This is not, by the way, a movie for family consumption). Reeves plays an up-and-coming lawyer who is being mentored and subtly corrupted by Pacino, whose character is a powerful lawyer and also, you guessed it, the devil himself.

The devil in this movie is named John Milton, the author of *Paradise Lost,* and is patterned after the character of Satan from that classic work.[10] His plan is to bring about Armageddon (of course) and to take over the world, but for some reason he needs the help of Reeves' character to do it. Reeves is hesitant to join the forces of the Father of Lies, largely because of the guilt he feels upon realising how far he has compromised his values.

The devil, in his recruiting effort, calls guilt a load of bricks, and refers to God as a prankster, a sadist, an absentee landlord, something he would never worship. He concludes by asserting that the twentieth century belongs entirely to him.

The devil is very persuasive, but it is evident throughout the whole speech that he is lying. Thus, there is a ring of authenticity to the performance. While we must be cautious not to make too many concrete statements about the devil – the information on him in the Scriptures is relatively scant – we do know that he has set himself in opposition to the King of Kings, and that Pacino's speech is the kind of thing we might expect to hear him saying. At the very least, we know that these sentiments belong securely to the kingdom of this world.

→ So wrong, so right? Bart Campolo is the President of Mission Year, a national Christian service programme that recruits young adults to serve in outreach teams that live and work in inner-city neighbourhoods. He tells the following story about a young inner-city kid called Tyrone, who came to Bart for help after being thrown out of his home.

I asked him what was going on. What had he done? Why was his mother throwing him out? By now he was crying, but eventually the story came out.

'She's throwing me out because I won't bust up the kid who lives across the hall from us. We just found out the boy's been raping my little brother, so now she wants me to hurt him bad so he don't do it no more. But I told her Bart says that Jesus says you can't be hurting other people like that, so she threw me out.'

I was stunned. I knew Tyrone's little brother. He was in our day camp, though he had barely smiled or said a word since it started. I told Tyrone we needed to call the police.

'Come on, Bart! You been 'round here long enough to know better than that.'

In the projects, I was learning, things worked differently. While I had been raised to trust police officers, Tyrone had been raised to fear them, for good reason. He was always showing me ways the system was broken here. In this case, it fell to Tyrone's mother to protect her little boy. Now I understood her anger too.

'You tell me what to do', he said.

I had no good answer, and both of us knew it. There was no good answer. I believe in Christian non-violence. It is wrong to send a kid out to bust up another kid. Then again, it is wrong to let somebody rape your little brother.

'Go and find that boy, Tyrone', I said. 'You go find him, and you hurt him. Hurt him so bad that he never comes near your brother again, do you hear?'

And then I went back to my house and I got down on my knees and asked God to forgive me. Through that encounter I realised that in the real world, the choices are not always between right and wrong; but sometimes between bad and worse.

I would not dare to suggest a singular definition of the kingdom of God, but I am certain of this much: a child will grow up there without ever having to sin to save his brother.

Bart Campolo[11]

THINGS TO DO

Read C. S. Lewis' *The Screwtape Letters*.[12] It is a short, creative, and eminently readable work of fiction which examines the tactics of the enemy and the counter-moves of the kingdom of God.

PLACES TO GO

The enmity between humanity and Satan – Genesis 3:15
The armour we need in the battle – Ephesians 6:10-20
The hatred of the devil – Revelation 12:17-13:1
A friend of the world is an enemy to God – James 4:1-5
Those who do not join in the battle are actually fighting on the enemy's side – Luke 11:23

3.3 A Tale of Two Cities – The Mismatch

LOCATION: *'As the weeds are pulled up and burned in the fire, so will it be at the end of the age. The Son of Man will send out his angels, and they will weed out of his kingdom everything that causes sin and all who do*

> evil. They will throw them into the fiery furnace, where
> there will be weeping and gnashing of teeth. Then the
> righteous will shine like the sun in the kingdom of their
> Father. He who has ears, let him hear' (Mt. 13:40-43).

We looked in the last section at the contrast between the kingdom of
God, represented by Jesus in the manger, and the kingdom of the world,
represented here on earth by one such as Caesar Augustus in Rome. The
question now is: where does the real power and glory lie? In the world?
Or in the manger?

Caesar Augustus causes the known world to be counted in his census;
the birth of Jesus causes the angels to sing in the heavens. Augustus
alters the course of a young couple's lives, making them journey to Beth-
lehem for the birth of their Son; the birth of that Son alters the course
of world history forever. Augustus uses the threat of his armies to force
a temporary peace amongst men; Jesus uses obedience, humility and
suffering to bring about an eternal peace between God and humanity. It
is under the authority of another Caesar that Jesus is put to death; that
death, and the subsequent resurrection, makes salvation possible for all
who would call Jesus Lord. Augustus and Rome reflect all the glory of the
kingdom of the world; Jesus reflects all the glory of the God who made
the world. Jesus shows us that the world's understanding of power and
glory is flawed. Real power and glory are found in obedience, sacrifice,
humility, grace, justice, love, and forgiveness. This is the power and
glory that exist in the kingdom of God.

So we see in the life of Jesus a potent alternative to the kingdom of
the world, an alternative to the rule of Satan. We also see in his parables
a glimpse of how God will ultimately deal with the challengers to his
throne. While we must acknowledge that there is still a battle to be
fought, that bullets are still flying, and people are still being wounded
and killed, we can say with confidence that the end result of the war is
not in question.

The best analogy I have heard for this is from the Second World War.
On D-Day, June 6, 1944, the Allies landed on the beaches of Normandy,
France. After a day of harrowing fighting, the beaches were taken, and a
massive beachhead was established through which soldiers, equipment

and supplies could be brought into mainland Europe. Once this had been accomplished, the war was effectively won. Germany had set its hope on being able to prevent a landing and sustained invasion into France, and it had failed. The Allied march to Berlin, while it would be costly, both in equipment and lives, was now a sure thing. The power of the Nazi regime had been broken. Yes, it could still do damage. Yes, nations still had to be liberated, battles still had to be fought. But victory for the Allies was ultimately secure.

The life, death, and resurrection of Jesus is humanity's D-Day, if such a term could even begin to describe the victory that is won over sin and death. Satan had set his hope on being able to prevent a landing and sustained invasion into the world, and he has failed, his power is broken. Yes, he can still do damage. Yes, there is still a costly battle to be waged, and people to be liberated. But Jesus affirms in our parable that he is the champion, and that at harvest time the righteous will be brought to him. The evil one and his children, on the other hand, will be destroyed.

This type of 'judgement' language seems harsh to our ears, but it is the ultimate example of 'Holy War'. God cannot, in the end, brook any rival, any enemy, any traitor to his kingdom. The offences of the devil and his followers are such that God's decisive action is not only justified — not that we are God's judge by any means — but inevitable. Psalm 24 tells us that 'The earth is the Lord's and everything in it.' So God must possess entirely what is rightfully his. Usurpers to the throne of creation will be disposed of with terrible judgement. He who has ears, let him hear: the King is victorious.

THINGS TO DO

Write down the things that count for power and glory in this world. Then write the things that count for power and glory in the kingdom of God. Pray that your life and the life of your church will find its identity in the kingdom of God.

Read Revelation 5:1-14. Jesus is described here as both a lion, and a slain lamb. What images do both of these descriptions bring to your mind? What do they tell you about the power and glory of Jesus?

NOTES FROM FELLOW TRAVELLERS

'Christ's love is always stronger than the evil in the world, so we need to love and be loved: it's as simple as that.'

Mother Teresa[13]

'Jesus shows no panic in the presence of evil. He does not give his seedword greenhouse protection. He is confident that good seed has vastly better survival strength than weeds.'

Eugene Peterson[14]

KINGDOM SIGHTINGS

'Laszlo Tokes, the Romanian pastor whose mistreatment outraged the country and prompted rebellion against the Communist ruler Ceausescu, tells of trying to prepare a Christmas sermon for the tiny mountain church to which he had been exiled. The state police were rounding up dissidents, and violence was breaking out across the country. Afraid for his life, Tokes bolted his doors, sat down, and read again the stories in Luke and Matthew. Unlike most pastors who would preach that Christmas, he chose as his text the verses describing Herod's massacre of the innocents. It was the single passage that spoke most directly to his parishioners. Oppression, fear, and violence, the daily plight of the underdog, they well understood.

'The next day, Christmas, news broke out that Ceausescu had been arrested. Church bells rang, and joy broke out all over Romania. Another king Herod had fallen. Tokes recalls, "All the events of the Christmas story now had a new, brilliant dimension for us, a dimension of history rooted in the reality of our lives.... For those of us who lived through them, the days of Christmas 1989 represented a rich, resonant embroidery of the Christmas story, a time when the providence of God and the foolishness of human wickedness seemed as easy to comprehend as the sun and the moon over the timeless Transylvanian hills." For the first time in four decades, Romania celebrated Christmas as a public holiday.'

Philip Yancey[15]

TOUR GUIDE

'God's kingdom means the divine conquest over His enemies... and the first victory has already occurred. The power of the kingdom of God has invaded the realm of Satan – the present evil Age. The activity of this power to deliver men from satanic rule was evidenced in the exorcism of demons. Thereby, Satan was bound; he was cast down from his position of power; his power was "destroyed." The blessings of the Messianic Age are now available to those who embrace the kingdom of God. We may already enjoy the blessings resulting from this initial defeat of Satan. Yes, the kingdom of God has come near, it is already present.'

G. E. Ladd[16]

PLACES TO GO

The kingdom of God is near – Luke 10:1-23
A promise of our power over demons – Luke 10:19
Kingdom of God versus Satan – Matthew 12:22-29
Defeating the power of death – Hebrews 2:14
Satan's fall from heaven – Revelation 12:7-12

3.4 A Tale of Two Cities – The Strategy

LOCATION: The servants asked him, 'Do you want us to go and pull them up?' 'No,' he answered, 'because while you are pulling the weeds, you may root up the wheat with them. Let both grow together until the harvest. At that time I will tell the harvesters: First collect the weeds and tie them into bundles to be burned; then gather the wheat and bring it into my barn' (Mt. 13:28b-30).

Part of the beauty of the parables is not in the answers that they give, but in the questions that they raise. Questioning is as much a part of human life as eating, breathing and sleeping. We all tend to navigate our way through life with a compass of questions, often challenging, sometimes unanswerable.

One of those questions which everyone has to face is the following: 'Why does so much bad stuff happen?' For those of us with a belief in an all-powerful and all-loving God, the answer to this question seems elusive. TV news screams 'Heresy!' at our doctrine. Our well-rehearsed arguments run out of steam. Our honest question fades into helpless petition: 'Why don't you do something?! If you're all good and all-powerful, come and take away the violence, the pain and the bad stuff!'

As we wait for an answer, nervous of being struck down, we gingerly lift our heads to heaven and wait for the sky to be ripped in two, hoping that lightening might carry angels on its electric charge; fantasising that the *Left Behind* fictions might be accurate in their apocalyptic imaginings. We dare to believe that in one almighty eschatological moment, the battle might be fought and won. That sin might be mopped up. That hope might be certain. That the kingdom might come, right now, in a blaze of glory, and that we might get to play a part as agents of God's mighty judgement.

This, of course, is not what we find as we walk through the parable of the weeds. When the farmer's men come to offer their help in the battle against the bad stuff, Jesus' response is emphatic: it is not the time for weeding out the bad, for the sake of the good. The darnel has become so embedded within the ecosphere of the field that to remove it would certainly destroy good wheat. Even worse, by this stage it has become impossible to tell the good from the bad. This is not what a desperate Israel wants to hear. As mentioned above, Israel has been waiting a long time for her God to act, to remove the evil and to reward the righteous. Israel wants angels, avenging angels. Israel wants justice, infinite justice for her sons who were massacred by a brutal foreign regime which bore no respect for her rights or her religion. Israel is yearning for a climatic harvest time.

It is so easy for us to want to call down the fire of heaven upon the unrighteous, just as John and James hoped for when they met opposition in Samaria (Lk. 9:54b). The problem is, while we think we can easily differentiate the good from the bad, our hearts know a different reality. The dilemma of sin and evil in the world cannot be dealt with by using human reason. It is not possible for us to isolate the bad for the sake of the good. The weeds of sin have become too intertwined with the very fabric of human existence.

Forgive me for another reference to the world of current affairs but I feel that the light of this parable must illuminate our thinking on recent events. In the aftermath of terrorist attacks and armed responses, the question is raised more starkly than before: 'How do we protect the good and get rid of the bad?' In the news reports of the last few years, I have seen a growing simplification of this eternally complex situation. I have heard talks of 'crusades' against the 'new evil' of this world. One prominent statesman has made the incredible statement that the present goal of his country is the 'eradication of evil'. The implication is that we can pinpoint the cause of evil to an individual or a group, and that by removing him or them from this plane of existence we can return the world to the 'peaceful harmony' it enjoyed prior to this current evil situation. I see the politicians and the public dividing the world up into goodies and baddies, or maybe even wheat and weeds. What's worse is that the pervading character of leadership is not that of the wise farmer but that of John Wayne. The ensuing shootout may get rid of some of the bad stuff, but it will almost certainly destroy much of the good with it.

Please read me right. I cannot and would not condone the heinous acts of terrorism we have seen around the world in recent years. I would also not dare to suggest that the solution to terrorism is to sit back and wait for things to get better. However, when I read of 'Operation Infinite Justice', I am given cause to consider all the crimes of my own nation, society and religion. I wonder whether this so-called infinite justice might stretch out and cover these wrongs. I suspect not. While such an operation may bring some terrorists to justice, I doubt that it will make recompense for the millions of people in the developing world who have paid for the luxuries of my life with their lives. I suspect that justice will not be done for the slaves who make my sports clothes in Asia or the peasants who farm my coffee in South America. I suspect that justice will not be done for the AIDS orphans of Africa who cannot afford the drugs that my government gives out for free. What's more, I know that justice will not be done for what Christians did to many thousands of Muslims in the crusades, and to millions of Jews throughout centuries of oppression. Nor for what many Christians do today, in blindly supporting an Israeli regime which continually oppresses Arabs of all faiths in the West Bank and the other occupied territories. The diplomatic way forward may seem clearer to some than others, but no matter what it brings, war or peace, reconciliation or annihilation, it certainly will not bring infinite justice to this world.

The parable of the weeds shows us that there is no point in sending out men into the fields to destroy the good for the sake of the bad. The good wheat and the poisonous weeds have grown so close that it is impossible to see where one stops and the other begins. Jesus realises that society is so steeped in sin as to make differentiation impossible. Sin is not the problem of one religion, region or race. Sin is the problem for the planet, and we are all as much part of the problem as we are potentially part of its solution. For the weeds to be taken away at this stage would require the destruction of the whole field, something God promised never to do again.

Clearly, the problem of sin and evil is a great one, and the strategy for sorting the wheat from the weeds must be terrifically complex and careful. Fortunately it is a problem which Jesus' kingdom does not ignore nor is impotent to overcome. The administration of infinite justice in this world does not rest with any political leader or group, whether we are talking about an Islamic terrorist, a political cowboy, a summit of powerful nations or a rock-star led coalition of anti-poverty campaigners. This job has been given to a wise and patient farmer, one who wields, as we saw earlier, 'left-handed power'. It is a power that will deal with the enemy and his influence in ways that we cannot imagine.

Typically, a Palestinian farmer faced with darnel will appoint his helpers to wander throughout the field and collect the crop. The workers must carefully and painstakingly cut each piece of wheat just a few inches beneath the ear for the harvest to be effective. Having gathered in every inch of wheat, the farmer sets fire to the remaining weeds and leaves his field clean once more. But Jesus' farmer takes an altogether different tack, once again leaving the textbook of agricultural techniques to one side. This farmer insists that the weeds be removed and thrown into the fire before the wheat is harvested and brought into his barn (Mt. 13:30).

This excursion into unreality provides no surprise for the parable lover.[17] A rabbi would often break from the bounds of reality in order to make his point. Such a manoeuvre alerts the listener to a new twist in the tale. Jesus and his audience both know that no farmer would try to remove the weeds from the wheat at harvest. This job would have been even more challenging than removing the ears of corn by hand, as the nature of the entanglement between the weed and the wheat would make separation almost impossible. But Jesus' farmer is emphatic: 'Collect the weeds and tie them in bundles to be burned; then gather the wheat and bring it to my barn' (Mt. 13:30). All the weeds are to be dealt with individually before any wheat is brought in.

Jesus' parable is as sophisticated a response to evil and suffering as any of us will ever find. Like the Jews, it may not be what we want to hear, but its apologetic offers a hope and a mystery beyond any man's imagination. It means that good and evil continue to co-exist in the short term, and that the two kingdoms will fight it out over time, but it also promises that the former will eventually and inexorably overcome the latter. This does not mean we shouldn't work for justice here and now, as justice is actually a fruit of the kingdom whose seed God has planted in the lives of his followers. We cannot claim to understand the kingdom and at the same time close our eyes to the suffering in the world. But the parable does tell us in no uncertain terms that victory — and vengeance — is ultimately in God's hands, not ours. And God's hands guarantee that no grain of good wheat will accidentally find its way into the fire at harvest time; the farmer's judgement is both complete and personal. Jesus' strategy does not provide a quick fix but rather an eternal solution. He does not deal in temporary vengeance but rather in true and infinite justice.

 NOTES FROM FELLOW TRAVELLERS

'Often it seems that we have heard the invitation of Jesus to be humble, compassionate, and forgiving, to take last place, to carry our cross and lose our life as an invitation for our individual lives, our family lives, or our lives within the communities of prayer and service... But when it comes to the relationship among nations, when we are dealing with decisions that have implications for our nation's role in the world, when we are thinking about our national security and its political ramifications, then we suddenly reverse our attitude completely and consider the gospel demands as utterly naive. When it comes to politics, power is the issue, and those who suggest that the powerless way of Christ is also the way to which the nations are called find themselves quickly accused as betrayers of their country.'

Henri Nouwen[18]

'Our favourite solutions to the world's deep and humanly intractable problems with sin are punching people on the nose, locking them up in the slammer, and – failing all else – buying them a one-way ride out of town in the electric chair. Worse yet when we come to the point of giving God advice about how to deal eternally with the same problems, we simply concoct eternal variations of the same procedures.'

R. F. Capon[19]

Martyn Joseph, the well-known singer-songwriter, wrote the following song after a trip to the Third World. He came back with his faith both challenged and radicalised:

Locked in my heart there's a child
Knocking the door to get out
He's asking the questions that hurt him
Sometimes it's a question of doubt
I can't pretend that it's easy
I can't pretend that I win
When your search in this life is over
That's when the struggle begins

And if I don't find out,
The search is not in vain
And if I don't find out
I hold on and I

Treasure the questions
As they rage in my mind
And I treasure the questions
Some day I will find
You know I ran out of answers
Such a long time ago
And I treasure the questions
Wherever I go.

Searching Saharas of sorrows
Trying to understand why
The journey has drawn me
So much closer
I don't have to stand here and lie
Over and over I cried in the darkness
Over and over to see
The crime is to sit and not wonder
Renewing my mind set me free

And if I don't find out,
The search is not in vain
And if I don't find out
I hold on and I

Treasure the questions
As they rage in my mind
And I treasure the questions
Some day I will find
You see I ran out of answers
Such a long time ago
And I treasure the questions
Wherever I go.[20]

KINGDOM SIGHTINGS

→ *The Shawshank Redemption* is a film adaptation of a Stephen King short story, and it is one of my all-time favourite movies.[21] It tells the story of Andy Dufresne, a man who spends most of his adult life in the Shawshank penitentiary for a crime he did not commit. Andy is different from the other long-term prisoners, like his friend Red, in that he refuses to become 'institutionalised'. This is in spite of the fact that he suffers enormous injustice and has no realistic hope of reprieve. He continually strives to remind his fellow inmates of the fact that there is a reality outside of their prison walls, and that they must hold onto hope. It is a struggle, however, to communicate this powerful message to a group of inmates who see no reason for hope.

→ The persecuted kingdom.

Believers in North Korean political prison camps face brutal treatment, torture and execution for their faith in Christ. They have suffered for half a century under a regime which views a belief in God as a direct challenge to its authority.

Christian Solidarity Worldwide has various reports on the ill-treatment of believers at political prison camps, including an incident where a guard poured a white-hot liquid iron over Christians as a punishment for refusing to renounce their faith. Christian inmates in these camps are forced to keep their faces towards the ground to stop them looking up to God, often leading to permanent deformity.

Christian mothers face the heartbreaking ordeal of being separated from their children who are then put into cages for the rest of their childhood. Each morning mothers are forced to walk past these cages where they can see their children, hungry, cold and neglected. Christians are kept in these camps for as long as they keep their faith. If they renounce Christ, they can walk free at any time. Prison guards are promoted for 'rehabilitating' prisoners, giving them an added incentive to target Christians for beatings, torture, harsh labour and rape. It is a testimony to the power of grace that the faith of these believers survives at all.

A former prisoner who was not a Christian at the time of her imprisonment told CSW: 'They had such a warm love that the rest of the people didn't know. I have seen and felt that even in such a difficult situation they were able to express love for others. They sometimes even took responsibility for others' wrongdoing. They took the blame to protect others! I realised that they are living in a different world, experiencing a different level of love. One of the reasons I have survived up to this moment is because of them. I reflect back and keep it as a guide, remembering them as they gave up their lives for the kingdom of God with the type of love that all Christians should have.'

Richard Chilvers[22]

THINGS TO DO

Rent the movie *The Shawshank Redemption* and note the places in the story which reflect something of the kingdom of God, particularly in terms of justice and hope.

Then pray for the persecuted church, that those Christians who are suffering for their faith would be able to hold onto the hope of Jesus, and the promise of infinite justice.

Educate yourself as well on the issues facing the persecuted Church, and see what you may be able to do to help. Find information at www.csi-int.org

---

USEFUL WORDS AND PHRASES

Mishpat: noun – Hebrew, tr. justice.
Hesed: noun – Hebrew, tr. steadfast love.
Shalom: noun – Hebrew, tr. peace.

Mishpat is a Hebrew word meaning justice. This justice does not refer to a strict interpretation of the letter of the Law, but conveys instead the concepts of morality, equality and righteousness. *Mishpat* was the system of justice that God wanted instituted in the nation of Israel, as we can see through such laws as the Year of Jubilee.

Mishpat is closely related to another Hebrew word, *hesed*, which can be translated as 'steadfast love.' We can see *hesed* at work in the compassionate laws instituted by God, whereby the poor would be taken care of by the wealthy. *Mishpat* guarantees justice, *hesed* deals with the spirit with which we administer that justice.

Both words are linked with the final Hebrew term, *shalom*. The word can be translated as 'peace', but the actual meaning of the word conveys the concepts of wholeness, harmony, and balance, in nature, social relations, economics and the spiritual life. *Shalom* defeats greed, selfishness, hatred, injustice, and anything else that would disrupt the proper peace that God wishes us to have.

All three of these terms are essential in the understanding of Jesus' ministry, and of his plan for the ultimate defeat of evil.[23]

TOUR GUIDE

Who is the sower in the first three kingdom parables (sower, wheat and tares, and mustard seed)? We have already identified as a misreading the typical interpretation of the church sowing the word of God through its preaching and evangelism. That leaves us with few other options. Most commentators, such as Robert Gundry, seem to suggest that the sower is Jesus, although some resist identification or go with the Father. Robert Farrar Capon is very clear on who he thinks the sower must be, and he comes to his conclusion by focusing on what the sower is planting – the word of God.

'The primary meaning of the phrase the Word of God in the New Testament, and in Christian theology as well, has got to be one that is consistent with the Johannine teaching that the Word is the one who was in the beginning with God and who is, in fact, God himself... above everything else, the Word has to mean the eternal Son – God of God, Light of Light, True God of True God – the Second Person of the Holy and Undivided Trinity. Do you see what that says? It says, first of all, that the sower is God the Father, not Jesus. What Jesus turns out to be – since he is the Word – is the seed sown.'

R. F. Capon[24]

PLACES TO GO

The weeds binding the wheat – Romans 2:1-4
God's incredible power and promise of judgement – Nahum 1:3-8
Good seed will not produce bad fruit. We are known as sons of the kingdom by the fruit we produce – Matthew 7:20

1   R. T. France, *New Testament profiles: Matthew, evangelist and teacher* (Illinois: InterVarsityPress, 1989) p225

2   J. F. MacArthur Jr., *The gospel according to Jesus* (Grand Rapids: Zondervan Publishing House, 1988) p130

3   *New Bible Dictionary* eds J. D. Douglas and N. Hillyer (Leicester: IVP, 1982) p984

4   J. F. MacArthur Jr., *The gospel according to Jesus* (Grand Rapids: Zondervan Publishing House, 1988) p131

5   J. F. MacArthur Jr., *The gospel according to Jesus* (Grand Rapids: Zondervan Publishing House, 1988) p132

6   John Milton, *Paradise Lost* edited J. Leonard (London: Penguin, 2000)

7   N. T. Wright, *Jesus and the victory of God* (London: SPCK, 1996) p451

8   N. T. Wright, *Jesus and the victory of God* (London: SPCK, 1996) p443

9   *The Devil's advocate* (Warner Home Video, 2001)

10 John Milton, *Paradise Lost* edited J. Leonard (London: Penguin, 2000)

11 Bart Campolo, *Kingdom Works* (Michigan: Servant Publications, 2001) p52

12 C. S. Lewis, *The Screwtape Letters* (London: Fount, 1977) pp39-40

13 Mother Teresa, *Meditations from a simple path*, excerpted from *A simple path*, compiled by Lucinda Vardey (New York: Ballantine Books, 1996) p36

14 E. Peterson, *Praying with Jesus* (San Francisco: Harper San Francisco, 1993)

15 Philip Yancey, *The Jesus I never knew* (Grand Rapids: Zondervan Publishing House, 1995) p40

16 G. E. Ladd, The gospel of the kingdom: Scriptural studies in the kingdom of God (Grand Rapids: W. B. Eerdmans Publishing Co., 1959) p50

17 R. H. Gundry, *Matthew: a commentary on his handbook for a mixed church under persecution* (Grand Rapids: W. B. Eerdmans Publishing Co., 1994) p256

18 Henri Nouwen, *Seeds of hope: a Henri Nouwen reader* edited by Robert Durback (Toronto: Bantam Books, 1989) p184

19 R. F. Capon, *The parables of the kingdom* (Grand Rapids: W. B. Eerdmans Publishing Co., 1985)

20 Martyn Joseph, taken from the *Full Colour Black and White album*, ALD074 www.martynjoseph.com

21 *The Shawshank Redemption* (Cinema Club, 1997)

22 Richard Chilvers, Communications Manager, Christian Solidarity Worldwide, www.csw.org.uk

23 Richard Foster, *Streams of living water: celebrating the great traditions of the Christian faith* (San Francisco: HarperSanFrancisco, 1998) pp169-172

24 R. F. Capon, *The parables of the kingdom* (Grand Rapids: W. B. Eerdmans Publishing Co., 1985) p69

CHAPTER 4

KINGDOM EXPANSION

The Parables of the Mustard Seed and the Yeast – Matthew 13:31-35

Historically, a kingdom's 'foreign policy' is often just a euphemistic term for 'taking over other countries'. A strong kingdom is not always interested merely in defending its territory; it wants to extend its borders, conquer new lands and fly its flag in distant and exotic locations.

The Bible says a lot about the expansion of the kingdom of God. In some places the focus is on the human side of the equation; how God's people are allowed and expected to be involved in the great kingdom work. But the parables of the mustard seed and the yeast in Matthew 13 show us a different image. The emphasis here is strongly, maybe even exclusively, on God's sovereignty. Here we see God alone assuming the responsibility for the extension of his kingdom. How these two aspects of kingdom building — human action and divine sovereignty — fit together is a paradox, an eternal mystery. But this mystery is a landmark of the kingdom you are travelling in.

4.1 What is a Soldier to do?

> *LOCATION: He told them another parable: 'The kingdom of heaven is like a mustard seed, which a man took and planted in his field'* (Mt. 13:31).

Having recovered from the exhaustion of harvest time, the sower is once more brought out onto the stage. This time the farmer is working with a mustard seed. The symbolic location of the parable remains unchanged: an ordinary field for our ordinary world. The basic plot and theme of our story are also familiar. This is a historical account, a description of what God has already done in the world. 'The kingdom of heaven is like a mustard seed, which a man took and planted in his field.' But this time the kingdom is not in countless sacks or handfuls of seed thrown freely over the whole field. The kingdom here is like a mustard seed. It is focused, unified, singular and whole. Above all, it is small.

The first surprise, though, is not the size of the seed; it is the size of the cast. Apart from the farmer planting, the story lacks any human touch. If we interpret the sower in this parable as God or Jesus, as must certainly be the case, then no ordinary man or woman features in the plot at all. It is for this reason Brad Young suggested that the parable of the mustard seed is unique among Jewish parables.[1] Where are all the people?

The lack of actors in this drama presents a serious challenge for all travellers seeking to understand the story. Parables usually work because they are interactive. They are not like the discussions of the priests and the Pharisees, which take long lists of laws and expound them with abstract concepts from philosophy and theology. Parables are more imaginative and creative. They are used to bring the Torah to life, to access the inaccessible, and to excite an audience with the purpose and person of God. Fundamental to this process is the parable's ability to draw the audience into the plot. Parables are akin to a virtual reality experience which requires the audience to jump in and live the life of the characters. What would they do if they were in this position? Where would they stand in such a dilemma? How would they feel if this was them?

The parables discussed in the previous two chapters were not chock-full of characters to choose from, but at least there were wheat, weeds and farm hands to grab hold of. With no one to watch in this parable, whom can we relate to? Again, we cannot claim to be the man who sowed the seed. This is surely God, and even if it isn't, whoever he is, he has been and sown and gone before we got here. So if we are not included in the plot, then hasn't the parable lost its power? Even more worrying, does it mean that we are not to be involved in the story of the growth of the kingdom?

In my tradition this parable seems especially troubling. Kingdom theology is part of our roots in the Salvation Army. William and Catherine Booths' mission was born out of their passionate all-pervading vision of the kingdom. Their job was not to build a church or raise up a new denomination.

Their founding dream instead was of the kingdom extended around the world. They envisioned the kingdom in every land, in every town and in every social grouping. The kingdom where it was needed most, 'in lowly cot and stately home.'[2] Nothing else would 'meet the hunger of their souls' but to see the whole world won for God's kingdom.[3]

Such a vision was news to me. As a child of the regiment, I remember that the kingdom made two appearances at every service. Both were brief and unexplained. The first followed the words, 'Now let us join in the prayer that Jesus taught us...' The ensuing rendition of the Lord's Prayer came and went. Somewhere in the monotone rhythm of the congregation the word *kingdom* appeared, but it soon dissipated into the routine rumble of the rest. The second regular mention of the kingdom was altogether more intriguing. Having taken the offering, a strange ritual would commence, a semi-sacred procession. The choreographed pacing and placing of collection plates provoked another prayer. This time audience participation was not allowed. 'Dear Lord,' the prayer would begin 'we thank you today for all that you have given us. In gratitude, we offer these gifts back to you and pray that you would use them for the extension of your kingdom.'

'So the kingdom is the thing that happens after the collection,' I thought to myself. My interpretation was further impeded by my definition of the word 'extension.' For me, such a noun was all wrapped up in the vocabulary of DIY and home improvements; after all my parents were always banging on about the possibility of building an 'extension'. 'Was that really what the offering went towards?' I wondered. 'Was my humble church helping God to build an addition onto his dream home?' I could never quite conceive as to why God, as king of heaven and earth, and the one careful owner of space and time should need a conservatory, a larger kitchen or an extra bedroom. Maybe he wanted a games room. Now I could relate to that. Somewhere to put a pool table but big enough for the odd game of indoor football. This was the kind of 'extension' that a kid could get his head around. But surely heaven was already kitted out with such necessities?

The place of the kingdom has obviously been greatly reduced in Salvation Army theology and practice. As we have grown up, we have become entangled in the administration of an international denomination and social services operation. While much of this has been inevitable and good, the founding dream has, at times, become tarnished, revised or even forgotten. In addition, the twentieth century taught us that some of what passed for nineteenth century kingdom theology was not so much theology as wishful thinking. The United Kingdom was not the kingdom of God on earth and the British Empire was not the key to the completion of the Great Commission. Some elements of this theology have survived the forgetfulness and revision of history. We still aim our giving at the extension of the kingdom. We volunteer our time, our money, our talents and our strategy in the hope that somehow God's kingdom will be extended. Not long ago, the Territorial motto for the Salvation Army in Canada was 'Do Something!' It was not exactly clear what should be done, but the fear was that if it didn't get done, the kingdom would not get any larger.

For this reason many of us in the Salvation Army, as well as in the larger body of evangelical churches, will find the message of the parable of the mustard seed surprising, even unwelcome. This parable shakes us from the false expectation that our efforts can establish or grow the kingdom of God. The sower comes, the sower plants, the sower leaves, and the tree grows. We can never pretend to be the sower, for this would be to play God. 'So what is left for us to do?' we ask. The answering silence deafens. Can it be that there is nothing for us to do?

The kingdom, oddly enough, seems to belong to the King. It is his to plant and his to grow. It begins with him, it remains with him, and it ends with him. The kingdom is not in *need* of our offering, and it does not *require* our intervention. It is as silly to presume that we are decisive to its being, as it is to suggest that we could build an extra bedroom on to the edge of time and space. If any extensions are to be made to the kingdom, God is more than capable of taking care of it himself. Once again, I seem to be in danger of writing myself out of a job.

THINGS TO DO

Pray the following prayer: My aim is to be known by God, and to come to know him. To be loved by God, and to come to love him. To be, before I do. To live my life in a perpetual state of obedient, sacrificial, merciful worship. To be single-minded in my desire to be part of God's kingdom, and to allow this depth with God – and not my 'own' skills – to be the focal point of God's ministry through me. To reflect the light of Christ, and not to promote myself. To take hold of the life Christ offers – both the suffering and the glory – and to live it to the full.

Discuss with a friend what this prayer, if you were to live it out, would mean practically for your life. What changes would you have to make?

NOTES FROM FELLOW TRAVELLERS

'There is no way that anyone can force the turning of the wheel of history to bring about the kingdom. All such attempts have failed, and some instances have been demonic. Sin affects all attempts at righteousness for the self or for society... Neither Christians nor anyone else can build the kingdom. At best persons can align themselves with the future of God as they see it, but knowing that they must not confuse their convictions with the absolute will of God. God will bring about the kingdom. Waiting in patience does not mean being absolutely passive. But it does mean that we realise that God's purposes are greater than our own.'

A. J. Hultgren[4]

PLACES TO GO

God did not need the sacrifices of the Israelites, any more than he needs our help in building the kingdom – Psalm 50:7-15.

KINGDOM SIGHTINGS

I have to admit, it all looked rather dodgy. 'Dodgy', I had discovered from my time in London, is a British slang word – an adjective – which means 'a little off ', or 'a bit suspicious'; an egg salad sandwich that sits out on the counter for a day or two might be considered dodgy. The word can also be descriptive of someone's character, as in: 'That mobster/con man/lawyer seemed a little dodgy. Perhaps we shouldn't give him access to our bank account.'

In my case, the whole situation could be considered dodgy. My friend and I, both males in our early twenties, were wandering the streets of Soho, in London, our eyes scanning and appraising all the sights and sounds that assailed us. Soho is the area of London that is most readily identified with the sex trade. It is an oppressive assortment of sex shops, strip joints, male and female prostitutes, pimps, drug dealers, and yuppie-style restaurants (couldn't quite figure that one out), all operating openly and unashamedly, at all hours of the day. One could literally walk down a street and pass a massage parlour, an up-scale, outdoor eatery with a pretentious name like Chez Marco, and a girl who could not be older than sixteen offering you her body. If you happened to glance up to the second story of any of the buildings, you would probably see people in various stages of undress conducting diverse illegal transactions.

It was not actually an unusual sight, then, to see two young men walking the streets of Soho with interest etched into their faces. If you knew that these two young men were missionaries for the Salvation Army, however, then perhaps you can see the potential for 'dodgy-ness'. I am happy to report that we did not answer any of the siren calls to contribute to the burgeoning sex trade economy, though we received many offers. We were there to pray.

My friend Phil and I were members of the Salvation Army UK Mission Team, a group of dedicated young Salvationists who want to learn about mission and put it into practice. The motto of the team is: 'Reaching the unreached, training the untrained.' Our prayer-walks through Soho were meant to contribute to the reaching of the unreached: in this case, those people who made a 'living' off of the sale and/or destruction of the human body. We were assigned to help out a Salvation Army centre near Soho one day a week. Our desire, being young, energetic missionaries, was to parachute into Soho, pull sinners out, and get them miraculously saved through the power of Jesus and the magnetism of our personalities. We were somewhat disappointed when, upon asking the workers at the centre what they would like us to do, the answer we received was: 'Go and pray.'

So we walked and watched and prayed through the dirty streets of Soho, week after week, regularly rebuffing solicitations from young girls and strip club owners. At the end of each walk we would get some water to drink, as if to cleanse from our minds the images we had taken in and prayed for. We were sincere with our prayers; we prayed particularly that the power of God would break into Soho through the haze of sin and despair that seemed to hover over it like a cloud. But we couldn't help feeling a little powerless, and I regret to say, a little under-used. We were missionaries, walking around sin-central, and we were instructed not to talk to the people there, but rather to cover them in prayer.

Several weeks of this went by, and the 45-minute trip out to Soho on the Underground was becoming less and less thrilling. But one day upon our arrival at the centre, we were greeted by an very enthusiastic worker who had some incredible news to share. She told us how one of the workers at the centre whose job it was to walk around looking for people in need of shelter and food, was approached by an unkempt man off the street. The man, whom the worker did not recognise, walked straight up to him and asked: 'How do I become a Christian?' The worker was taken aback; this type of thing does not happen in Soho. Normally when an unkempt stranger approaches you in Soho the question is: 'How can I take your money at this time?' But the worker dutifully explained, as best he could, how the man could accept Jesus into his heart, and how he must recognise Jesus as Lord and Saviour of his life. Without any hesitation, the man did just that. And then, in the words of the worker: 'It was as if I could see the light of God breaking in through the dark atmosphere of Soho, and piercing straight into this man's heart'.

Phil and I were humbled. This man was not saved because of our 'evangelistic abilities', or our youth, energy, or cultural relevance. This man was saved because God is the King, and he chose to use our reluctant prayers to bring his light into one of the dark places of our world, light which could draw one unkempt man towards him. There is nothing dodgy about that.

4.2 Does Size Matter?

> *LOCATION: 'Though it is the smallest of all your seeds, yet when it grows, it is the largest of garden plants and becomes a tree, so that the birds of the air come and perch in its branches' (Mt.13:32).*

'The mustard seed was the smallest of Palestinian seeds that could be seen with the naked eye.'[5] If a first century Jew wanted to emphasis the miniature, he would call upon the analogy of the proverbial mustard seed. In a world without microscopes the mustard seed is one half of an atom; no mind could possibly conceive of anything smaller. 'Your brain is as big as a mustard seed' would be the perfect put-down. But it would also be a cunning compliment, for what the mustard seed lacks in size it makes up for in speed. The mustard seed grows quickly. No sooner is it in the ground than it sprouts forth and forms a plant.

In the past Jesus' sowing technique has seemed questionable. Some-where along the line, however, his thumbs have turned a strange shade of green. Jesus' mustard seed avoids convention, bypasses the bush phase of horticultural development and quickly becomes a mighty tree. No mention is ever made in Jewish literature of such a floral phenomenon. The mustard plant is, after all, only a herb. While it could grow to twelve feet tall, it would never have an entry in *The Big Blooming Book of Trees*. Yet Jesus' seed becomes a tree within a year of being planted.

With the picture of birds nesting in its branches, Jesus stretches our imaginations even further. A decent sized mustard plant might well have provided enough shelter for the odd bird who was brave enough to build his nest on terra firma, but it would never provide branches strong enough to hold multiple dwellings. The news that this picture may be a sequel to the visions of Ezekiel adds an even more fantastic wrinkle to the story (Ezek. 17:23). For the exiled prophet, the birds represented the nations of the world flocking to find their Creator and King in the almighty tree of Israel. Jesus borrows directly from these images. So now we are faced with the fact that it isn't just the odd bird, but actually the nations of the world living in the branches of Jesus' miracle mustard tree. This picture, as monstrously exaggerated and as cosmically distorted as it appears, is the promised happy ending of the kingdom.

Exaggeration like this is indispensable to the ancient art of communication. Those of us who score high on evangelism as a spiritual gift inevitably score high on exaggeration as a character trait as well. We can take the smallest acts of spiritual insignificance and turn them into signs of the kingdom, words to the nations, and the four horsemen of the apocalypse, all rolled into one. We blow our nose and all of a sudden it is the wind of the Spirit. Many meagre stories have been transformed by preachers to the point where they become known across the land as the greatest spiritual events since Pentecost. I have a friend who speaks all over the world and loves stealing my stories. The problem is that once he's in on the act, the story starts mysteriously evolving. Simple and accurate narration gives way to a one player game of Chinese whispers. Within a year metamorphosis is complete. Not one facet will remain the same and the now unchained tale is entirely free from any notion of reality. I would say something about it if I wasn't guilty of the self-same crime on an almost daily basis. In fact, one of Jesus' own examples of rabbinic exaggeration springs to mind when he said, 'Remove the log from your own eye before you point to the speck in mine' (Mt.7:2-5).

But exaggeration can be useful. The parable of the mustard seed gives us a marvellous insight into what we might call 'rabbinic exaggeration.' The growth of the tree in the story requires its audience to make a leap of imagination akin to that performed by an Olympic triple jump champion. But the story also demonstrates some delicious divine understatement. The mustard tree as described by Jesus is actually and metaphorically minute compared to the kingdom. The kingdom of God would dwarf even the greatest of trees.

In human terms, the oversized story destroys all sense of proportion. In Sunday school we would re-enact this story by taking some water cress seeds — mustard seeds not being available — and planting them on some soggy sheets of kitchen roll. The whole class would be subject to a united intake of breath the next week when we discovered that the seeds had grown into plants, four or five millimetres in height. It is only now that I realise just what a meaningless object lesson that was. If we had returned a week later and found a big oak tree protruding violently through the roof of the Sunday school hall, complete with tyre-swings, tree houses and nests of eagles in its branches, that would have been impressive. And while it would have been a huge oversized surprise of parabolic proportions, it would still have been an underestimate of what God intends to do with the kingdom. The kingdom starts small, but no sooner does it disappear into the ground than it starts to grow. Within no time at all, it has expanded beyond the bounds of the most overactive imagination. Think about the biggest thing you've ever seen, times it by one thousand and what you've got is still only a mustard seed in comparison with the size of the kingdom.

Underestimating God is something of an existential hazard. Just when we think we've got him sussed, he comes along and shows us that he's a whole lot bigger and better. As we underestimate the size and the nature of God, so too we underestimate the scope of his kingdom plans. Jesus' plan is not limited to making the world a better place. His ultimate vision is not one of a broken creation undergoing its annual service and repairs, nor of a diseased planet being prolonged in its sickened existence by a drip-feed of spiritual antibiotics. Neither is Jesus' plan limited simply to the restoration of our world. His hope is not that we all return to the Garden of Eden, minus our fig leaves. Jesus' plan is for the perfection of creation. Eden is not enough; the aim is to go one better. The vision is for a new heaven and earth to exceed all expectations, hopes and dreams of what is possible with this fallen world. The miracle of the kingdom is that a sinful world is being made more perfect than its perfect prototype.

That God can create perfection out of our imperfection seems hard to grasp in itself. But the notion that he can create a new and improved version of perfection seems almost contradictory. Imagine it this way: a few hundred years ago an artist called Michelangelo searched high and low for the most perfect slabs of marble. Having subjected his chosen material to every conceivable test of sight and touch, he would pronounce it to be perfect. It was only then that the sculptor would begin his work. With skill, artistry and imagination Michelangelo would begin the nearly impossible task of perfecting the perfect. Through the sweat and tears of time and effort, the sculptor would create hitherto unimaginable beauty from the beautiful material of God's creation.

Jesus' parable of the mustard seed shows us the master artist making his creation into something it never thought it could be. The kingdom is the perfection of creation, a perfection that was in the mind of the Father from the very first day. Not fallen human beings, cursed creation, nor the serpent himself can prevent the Creator from finishing what he has started. As we write, Jesus is making a new heaven and a new earth out of the old; a gigantic tree out of a tiny seed. These are not the wild exaggerations of evangelists and theologians. These are the stories of Jesus, the parables of the kingdom, and the reality of the Universe.

THINGS TO DO

It really is impossible for us even to contemplate the size or growth rate of the kingdom of God. How can temporal, physical, fallible creatures actually get their minds around a perfect kingdom, or Creator, neither of which are bound by time or space? Which is why Jesus had to use such an imperfect metaphor to try and get something of the kingdom across. I am not going to suggest that you plant anything in your garden to watch it grow; as mentioned above, this does not really get to the heart of the parable. Instead, I suggest you go to a place where there is something that overwhelms you with its size. You can try a forest with mammoth trees, a mountain if one is close by, the ocean or a huge lake, or even a tall skyscraper. Whatever is available.

Once there, take some time to meditate on Psalm 102:15-28, or any other Scripture of your choosing that demonstrates the awesome greatness of God. Continue to pray through the passage until you have come to a realisation of how small and impermanent your surroundings really are, in comparison to the kingdom of God.

NOTES FROM FELLOW TRAVELLERS

'Because we are so eager to arrange for our own future, we of little faith close ourselves off from what, in fact, might be coming... We become midgets in a world of tiny things.'

Henri Nouwen[6]

PLACES TO STAY

'I keep looking, God, for the dramatic moment when I can engage in a glorious sacrifice for the faith; you keep presenting me with daily opportunities for belief and obedience and hope. Help me to forget my dreams of melodrama, and accept the reality of your kingdom.'

Eugene Peterson[7]

PLACES TO GO

The vision of the enormous tree that Jesus uses for his new parable – Daniel 4:10-12
More understatement as the kingdom and the King are described – Revelation 21

KINGDOM SIGHTINGS

The Reject Prom

John Carlson, a young Lutheran minister in Minnesota, gained attention and praise when he came up with the innovative idea that there should be a special party the night of the senior prom for those who did not have dates. All across America the night of the senior prom is a time of hurt feelings and deep depression for hundreds of thousands of high school kids. Not to have a date for the senior prom is to be publicly declared a reject. Everybody knows that those who can't get dates for the prom have to be losers. What is even sadder is that the sense of rejection and inferiority symbolised by being dateless on prom night has haunted these kids all through their school years. The prom simply provides the finishing blow.

So far as John Carlson was concerned, the prom was not the kind of party that Jesus would have liked. It was too exclusive to be Christian, in his opinion. It seemed to be reserved for the beautiful and the popular. So John planned an alternative to the prom for those whom "the system" had deemed losers and rejects. He called it the Reject Prom. Those who did not have dates were especially invited – and the kids loved it. The Reject Prom was held the same night as the senior prom and it turned out to be a real blow-out party that made the senior prom seem tamed and dull by comparison.

Once the thing got started, there was no stopping it. Each year the number attending this party for rejects grew. The party began to get press coverage. Timex Corporation gave watches to the kids who attended. Other companies joined in, and those who came to the Reject Prom were overwhelmed with interesting gifts and souvenirs. It wasn't long before some of the kids who could get dates and go to the prom decided not to. They preferred to join in the good time that the 'rejects' were having at their special party. What a great sign that the kingdom of God is among us. What John Carlson pulled off must have had the angels in heaven chuckling and our Lord smiling. It is just the kind of celebration that He ordered...'

Tony Campolo[8]

USEFUL WORDS AND PHRASES

Automate he ge karpophorei: Greek phrase tr. 'the earth bears fruit of itself.' The use of this phrase in the parable once again emphasises the divine context of kingdom growth. The growth of the kingdom is a divine mystery. The kingdom is planted and the kingdom grows. No scientific or agricultural analysis is necessary. The kingdom grows – that's the way it is. Put the kingdom somewhere and the fruit follows.

4.3 Local Cuisine

LOCATION: He told them still another parable: 'The king-dom of heaven is like yeast that a woman took and mixed into a large amount of flour until it worked all through the dough.' So was fulfilled what was spoken through the prophet: 'I will open my mouth in parables, I will utter things hidden since the creation of the world' (Mt. 13:33-35).

It is time for the sower to rest. But the narrator has not yet finished. This kingdom is unrelenting and the finale is a long way off. This is what the crowd wants to hear. Their anticipation, a heady mix of confusion and wonder, grows. We can almost here their corporate cry, 'Encore!' Jesus will duly oblige.

The interval between the parables is short but provides stage hands with enough time to change the scenery. The curtain rises on a new day, a new set and a new cast. The backdrop is an everyday kitchen. The character is an everyday housewife. The plot is one of everyday grind. The normality of the scene is surprisingly undramatic. The kingdom takes the part of the yeast, which the woman promptly hides amongst the rest of her ingredients.

This is where the drama begins. We escape from this scene of domestic routine into a cosmic game of hide and seek. R. T. France has suggested that the drama of Matthew's gospel could be divided into five separate acts. The third act is entitled 'The hiding of revelation' and we are now approaching its climax.[9] At first such a title would seem to court contradiction. How can revelation be revelation if it is hidden away? The whole point of revelation is that it belongs to the realm of the absolutely obvious! But think again. The world of revelation is closely connected to the world of hiddenness; one cannot get by without the other. Revelation, by its very nature, is not obvious to everyone. The very word implies a supreme, special and even secret kind of knowledge. Revelations rely on things that have never before been revealed. For me to claim that the world is round is hardly a revelation; it is a true statement, but it is unlikely to grab any headlines. However, when Galileo attempted to break the same story several hundred years ago, it was a revelation of immense and scandalous proportions. This news, no matter how real and true, was hidden from everyone except the brave scientist. Galileo's revelations were light years away from what the Pope and the public considered to be the absolutely obvious. That was the point; that is what made it a revelation. News unheard of, unthinkable, unwanted and now unhidden. Hiddenness and revelation are different sides of the same coin, and each side is marked with a sign of the kingdom.

The scene of this parable is many miles removed from the dramas of farm life which preceded it. This does not mean that the parable of the leaven is an interval or an excursion. Jesus is not attempting to keep the womenfolk interested or bidding to become the housewives' favourite, before returning to the more manly and meaningful metaphors of life on the farm. The parable is integral to the overall drama of the chapter. What's more, it is entirely consistent with what has come before and what is yet to come. Like any great playwright or storyteller, Jesus uses this change of scene to reveal something that has, up to now, been hidden. The sub-plot of the piece is taking centre stage.

The kingdom of God is like yeast which was hidden in some flour. The kingdom of God is like a mustard seed which was hidden in the ground. The kingdom of God is like good seed which was hidden in a field. The kingdom of God has been hidden. To a Jew whose faith is rocked by the absence of the kingdom, this news may come as some relief, an explanation of their predicament. But for those who believe that the kingdom must always be visible, obvious and overshadowing, this must come as a revelation, and very possibly as a stumbling block. The eternal consistency of the kingdom is that it begins in hiddenness. It eludes the eye and presents itself to faith. If we set out for the kingdom then we, like Abraham in Genesis and Christian in *The Pilgrim's Progress* must pack our bags and head resolutely to a place that cannot be reached by our own cleverness and logic. As Bono once said: 'It's a place that has to be believed to be seen.'

The hiding of the kingdom is not a ploy to diminish its power or influence, nor is it God's way of keeping his work private, pure or protected. The hiding of the kingdom is God's strategy for maximum impact. While the kingdom may remain invisible to the naked eye, its effect is all-pervading. Having worked the yeast into the moisture of the dough, the housewife stands back and watches a miracle happen. The yeast, having been overcome by the flour, begins to work its magic. While indistinguishable from the rest of the ingredients, it slowly expands and extends into every part of the mixture. And this is no small story we are talking about here. The woman has taken three measures of wheat flour for her recipe. This would make enough bread for over one hundred people, meaning that the housewife is obviously preparing for some kind of massive banquet that ordinarily would be quite beyond her. The size of this kingdom feast is clearly going to exceed all rational expectations.

In the same way, the yeast in the parable starts small, becomes hidden, but then grows beyond the scope of our imagination. This means that when we are looking for obvious signs and markers during the course of our travels in this great land, but discover nothing or next to nothing, we should not be discouraged. This is the way of the kingdom. It should never surprise us that the kingdom eludes our gaze or grasp, because that is an essential part of God's strategy. He has hidden it so that it can become a more pervasive part of the whole. He has buried his kingdom deep in the science, philosophy, geography, theology and imagination of the planet. He has worked his kingdom into the mixture of world history in such a way that it has affected everything that has been and ever will be.

God has been so successful in this game of hide and seek that it is quite often impossible for us to differentiate where the kingdom ends and the world begins. The kingdom is so immersed in the dough of this world that it often cannot be identified, let alone separated. Instead, the kingdom works its magic, the 'deep magic' so powerfully evoked by Aslan in C. S. Lewis' Narnia tales. It redeems, it restores, it reorders and it reveals. It pushes a fallen creation towards a raised perfection. It extends, stretches and transforms people and places into what they were created to be. The kingdom is at work everywhere and everywhere it is both hidden and revealed. In history the kingdom is hidden, dug deep in the soil of human existence and largely invisible to our eyes. Yet Jesus reveals in this most simple of dramas, mysteries that have been 'hidden since the creation of the world' (Mt. 13:35). More than this, Jesus reveals something of himself as the mystery of the world. He is the seed that must be buried for the kingdom to shoot up, as a tree that can house all the nations of the world in its branches, and he is the yeast that must be consumed if the kingdom is to expand to its proper size inside of us.

In Jesus we have tasted the bread of life. This is the kind of bread which can stretch to satisfy all people throughout all time. And so we have not only heard the housewife's story but we have tasted her produce. We have attended her banquet and met her guest of honour, feasted with the King and called him friend. We have experienced the sure and certain hope of this King who was, and is, and is to come. We have shared his last supper and now we long for the next, for we know that another great feast is being planned and prepared. The guest list is huge, covering from north to south and east to west. This is the kingdom of God, whose hidden nature is revealed to us by a woman baking bread.

PLACES TO GO

Usually leaven symbolises the pervasive power of evil (Ex. 12:15-20; 23:18; 34:21-26; Lev. 2:11; Mt. 16:5-12; 1 Cor. 5:6-8; Gal. 5:9). But sometimes it is associated with what is good (Lev. 7:13-14; 23:17). Here the unusual use of leaven with a good association not only emphasises the pervasive power of the kingdom of heaven but also agrees with the inclusion of publicans and sinners in the kingdom.[10]

NOTES FROM FELLOW TRAVELLERS

'If He were not Mystery, there would be no need for Revelation, or, more precisely, there would be no need for God to reveal Himself.'

John Paul II[11]

'I want one of those keys you win in video games, that allows you to blast through walls and reach the next level – to get to "the other side".'

Douglas Coupland[12]

THINGS TO DO

→ Rabbi Nathan of Nemirov, speaking about the Scripture verses affixed to the *Tallith,* the traditional Jewish prayer shawl, explains that 'when words, particularly those conveying the names of God, are inscribed upon physical objects of the world, these words send vibrations out into the physical world itself.'

M. Ouaknin[13]

Compare this to the observation made by one of Jesus' disciples: 'The Word became flesh and made his dwelling among us. We have seen his glory, the glory of the One and Only, who came from the Father, full of grace and truth' (Jn. 1:14).

It is clear that some of Jesus' followers were becoming aware that wherever Jesus went, he left the fingerprint of the Father. On a piece of fabric, write down all the names, words, or phrases that you can think of to describe Jesus. Wrap the fabric around your arm and wear it for a day, as a reminder and a symbol that God, through Jesus, has put his fingerprint on you.

→ Watch the movie *Babette's Feast,* a beautiful story which focuses on a banquet to which all are invited, foreshadowing the heavenly banquet that is to come. Some friends of mine like to prepare a surprise feast featuring food from around the world. Having invited some people around to watch the film they unveil their ready-made feast. They celebrate the great banquet when creation will come from the north, south, east and west to sit down and feast in the kingdom of God.

USEFUL WORDS AND PHRASES

Once more some of our translations prevent us from unlocking the plot. The key phrase which Matthew uses to reveal Jesus' sub-plot is obscured. Where we often read that the yeast was 'mixed' with the flour, Matthew informs us that the housewife 'hid' the necessary ingredient. That single word is the key to unlocking the subconscious of the audience. Suddenly what has gone unnoticed up until now is as clear as the nose on the housewife's face.

- -

KINGDOM SIGHTINGS

After the morning service was over, Jennifer, a young inner-city missionary, was flying high beneath the wings of God's great and glorious love for his children and she was flushed with joy. She walked out of that church positively determined to share God's love with any and all lost and needy people who happened to come across her path from that moment forward. She decided to purchase a large cup of coffee and to give that cup of coffee to the first homeless person she saw.

Jennifer walked only a few steps before she saw a wild-looking man in a battered wheelchair, rolling straight towards her. He was a black man, about fifty years old, wrapped in a worn and dirty army coat. She was a little bit scared, but excited as well. Smiling warmly, she moved towards him. Before she could say a word however, the man in the wheelchair angrily addressed her.

'I know what you're gonna do!' he snarled. 'You're gonna offer me that coffee, aren't you?'

Jennifer smiled again, nodded her head and held out her gift.

'Well, you can keep your coffee!' he barked. 'I don't need coffee! What I need is a dollar!'

She was stunned at first and then she was angry. She withdrew the coffee and walked around the man in the wheelchair. Under her breath she muttered, 'What you need is Jesus!'

The man wheeled himself around and shouted after her.

'What's that you said to me?' he demanded.

She turned back to face him.

'You think I don't know Jesus?' he shouted. 'Who do you think helps me push this wheelchair every day? Who do you think takes care of me out here? Jesus does, that's who! Just because I'm poor, you think that I don't know Jesus?' He reached out and pushed her away with both hands. 'Go on, you; get out of here!'

Jennifer turned away sobbing, embarrassed and ashamed of herself for being so insensitive. She had thought of herself as better than him just because she was better off. She rushed away, along the sidewalk.

Halfway down the block, the man caught up with her. Looking up, he spoke again, but this time his voice was soft.

'Why did you do that?' he asked quietly. Jennifer stopped and looked at him.

'Because I wanted to show you that God loves you, and that was the best way I could think of.'

'Oh,' he said. 'That was your mistake right there. You think that the only way to show people love is by giving them stuff. You take a lesson from old Saint James here. When I want to love people, I look 'em right in the eye and give 'em the biggest smile I can and say, "Hello there!"'

They spoke for a while, mostly about their mutual faith in Jesus. After a while James stopped and looked up at her. 'Jennifer, God told me something to tell you,' said James. He tapped on his chest. 'You see, Jennifer, love comes from in here. It isn't things you give. It comes from your heart.' He paused. 'Listen, It's easy to love people, but it's easy to hurt people too.'

Jennifer nodded.

'I love you, Jennifer,' said Saint James.

'I love you, too, James' said Jennifer.

She leaned over and hugged him, and he hugged her back. Then they went their separate ways.

Jennifer said, later, that the things she learned from James utterly changed her life and defined her year working in Chicago. I do not doubt her. After all, sometimes that is how the kingdom works.

Bart Campolo[14]

- -

4.4 Manifest Destiny – Directions to the Kingdom

 LOCATION: Matthew 13:31-35

'Manifest Destiny' is a term which has been used to describe American expansionist tendencies. At one point, many in the US felt it was the manifest destiny of their country to see the Stars and Stripes flying at the North Pole, and at all points in between. Fortunately for the noble, true-hearted, brave Canadians who stood in the way, their territory was not annexed and turned into the fifty-first state of the Union. (I may be biased).

The kingdom of God, on the other hand, has a manifest destiny that I very much want to be a part of, and it can be seen somewhat in the parables of the mustard seed and the leaven. Of course, we must always remember that these parables are not invitations to build the kingdom of God. To those of us with an addiction to action this will bring a mixture of shock and fear, or possibly relief. If we can get past these initial emotions, however, we will find something truly amazing in the remainder of the parables.

It seems to bother us that God's order, plans and intentions rest in the large part upon himself. A colleague of mine once remarked that 'we Christians are too scared to admit that over 90 per cent of what God is doing, he is doing behind our backs.' We somehow need to believe that God would be nowhere without us, when we know that simply isn't the case. What is remarkable is that God lets us participate in his work at all, especially considering our track record. This kingdom is not our kingdom, but Jesus lets us in on it anyway. Jesus considers us important and trustworthy enough to share with us his ultimate dream and scheme for all of history. In the parables of the mustard seed and the leaven, Jesus rolls out the blueprint for creation. He sets before us his plan to make all things new. He spills the beans on the greatest conspiracy of all time, and invites us to be co-conspirators.

Quite often, unfortunately, we human travellers think God's revealed plan for creation is all about some kind of Utopian society here on earth. The problem with Utopia is that it doesn't exist. Every attempt to create a heaven on earth has failed. Caesar Augustus, the American fathers, Queen Elizabeth I, Karl Marx and Joseph Stalin all tried to create their own slice of heaven on earth, only to find that it was as weak and as wanting as the one it replaced. Many men and women have packed their bags and set out for such a destination but none have ever arrived. Even today, Christians and Jews alike miss this point about the kingdom. In our efforts to see its coming, we look to the world of nation states and current affairs. We contribute to the state of Israel and bless the scattered Jews that they might return to the land of their forefathers. We hope that as we build and promote our own civilisations, the kingdom might be embodied in our nations and lands. But the perfection of Utopia creates a border that none can cross. Our fallen identity is soon spotted by her passport control, and the contraband of immorality and error in our baggage are soon exposed by the x-ray machines of her customs officials. Our perfect get-away has become too perfect and even we, its creators, cannot be granted a visa or smuggled in. Utopia, by its own definition, is a place that we are destined never to visit.

So the kingdom should not be confused with Utopia. The kingdom is not fantasy: it is real, it exists. The kingdom is not to be found in naive, futuristic *Star Trek* scenarios in which we all live in harmony through reason, science, goodwill and identical clothing. It is to be found instead in parables about a mustard seed, some bread and a banquet; in signs, prophecies and miracles: in the story of the King of Kings, his creation, his birth, his life, his love, his laughter, his pain, his suffering, his death, his resurrection, his ascension, his earth and his heaven. This is a story which has infiltrated deep into the present reality of this world. His kingdom is marked everywhere, and everywhere it makes its mark. While it may be difficult to see, nothing could be seen without it. This reality absorbs all other realities. As such, it is not really accurate to say that we have found the kingdom; the kingdom finds us, and everyone else for that matter.

The story is told of a new convert who was encouraged by an evangelist to give his father a copy of the Bible. Knowing that his father was far from sympathetic to the claims of Christianity, the convert exclaimed, 'I am worried about what my father will make of the Bible.' The evangelist thought a while and replied: 'Don't worry what your father will make of the Bible, worry about what the Bible will make of your father.'

I have lost count of the times when I have seen the hidden kingdom making something of our world. While watching a movie, reading a book, overhearing a conversation or witnessing an action, I am struck by an obvious kingdom presence. Is it because that human being has suddenly found the kingdom and sought to express it in their work, their art or their conversation? We mentioned earlier Stephen King's remarkable short story,

The Shawshank Redemption.[15] Was such a tale the result of Stephen King finding the kingdom? Certainly the kingdom of God found Stephen King. Whether he knows it or not, for a period of time the kingdom of God, hidden or revealed, got hold of his imagination and as a subject of that kingdom, he expressed its reality. *The Shawshank Redemption* is not a testimony to what Stephen King can do with the kingdom, but rather what the kingdom can do with Stephen King. It is a testimony to the power of the kingdom to locate, discover and consume the messed up, the hurting and the demonic. This is part of the remarkable nature of the kingdom. Just as the King never discriminates, neither does the kingdom. No part of the world's field is left unsown, no matter how stony, shallow or thorn-ridden. No part of the world's dough is left unleavened, no matter how stodgy, tasteless or impure. God's plan is simple: everyone must experience the kingdom. Not as unspoken reality, political possibility, or dreamed-up Utopia, but as the here and now of our dusty 'dailyness'.

The kingdom does not disappear into the realms of our fantasy or dissipate in our failure to live up to its standards. The kingdom is not too good to be true. On the contrary, it is so good that it is the truth, and can only belong to God — the root of all truth, goodness and beauty. The even better news is that we, the King's people, cannot be precluded from his kingdom by our imperfections. One simple request and the mark of his perfection will be stamped on our passports. We will gain entry not through our dreams, hopes, efforts, demands or inventions, but only by the King's intervention. We have been given a royal boon, an invitation to a regal banquet, an eternal garden party. His Majesty's passport officials are not trained in the art of interrogation, as there is no need for such perverse artistry in this kingdom. These officials are not the humdrum bureaucratic servants of a nervous state. They are angels who roll out red carpets for thieves in the night. Today in paradise such people have become princes. His customs officials throw up their hands in praise and thanksgiving as their x-ray machines slowly rust from their persistent unemployment. 'How is it that people who have travelled this far have no baggage?' they ask one another. Their question is not one of cynical suspicion but sincere celebration.

The kingdom has turned everything on its head. Donald Kraybill was right when he called this an *'Upside-Down Kingdom.'*[16] An upside-down kingdom naturally requires an upside-down travel guide. It is at this point, as we near the climax of our epic journey, that I must make good another confession. The premise of this book has been to enable you, the reader, to locate the kingdom. But the truth of the matter is this: while I encourage you to search for the kingdom under every nook and cranny of divine revelation and human experience, I must warn you that the kingdom will find you before you find it. While we may need the help of such imperfect travel guides as this, the kingdom does not. The kingdom has always had you in mind as part of its plan and order. The King came looking for you long before you had even heard his name or presumed his existence.

For Israel this is illustrated by the relationship between the king and the shepherd. The job of shepherd was the lowest, meanest occupation in Israel. These dirty, smelly keepers of the sheep had little to recommend themselves, but their work was necessary. A shepherd protected and nurtured one of the essentials of farm produce. His sheep would become the sacred meal shared in the home and the required sacrifice made at the Temple.

For Israel, there was also an inextricable link between the place of the shepherd and the person of the king. While seemingly not the job for those who wished to get ahead in the world, many of Israel's greats started out in this profession: Abraham, Moses, and most importantly David. As a shepherd, David prepared for God's kind of kingship. His studies in shepherding encompassed servanthood, artistry, heroism and sacrifice. His graduation in kingship was the embodiment of a living prophecy. In all his imperfection, he represented the perfect King that was, and is, and is to come. All of his other achievements pass into insignificance alongside his role as an icon through which Israel sees God's kind of king.

With this in mind hear the words of Jesus saying, 'I am the good shepherd.' The one who went looking for his sheep. The one who was not prepared to sacrifice a single sheep and so sacrificed himself. The shepherd who looks and finds, and dies for his sheep. This is the King of this world and the next. The kingdom is not a get-away destination which we find in the pages of a travel book. The kingdom is a come-and-get-us destiny which God has orchestrated since the dawn of time.

Time for one more revelation. Not only does the Shepherd King die for the sheep, but the sheep, unbelievably, are the inheritors of his kingdom. Christ has made it clear that the kingdom's destiny is manifesting itself inside the lives of the King's subjects. This is what Jesus meant when he said 'the kingdom of God is within you' (Lk. 17:21b). To follow Christ the Shepherd, and to subject ourselves to his rule and upside-down order, is to have eaten the bread made by the housewife in the parable. Maybe this is why she made so much bread in the first place. She wanted everyone to get a slice. And as we eat this bread of life, we are in fact consuming the kingdom of God. His dynamic rule and sovereign power is being exercised first and foremost in his subjects. The reformer Martin Butzer calls this 'subministration.' As we subject every aspect of our lives to God's way of seeing, ruling and ordering things, we re-administrate our lives to reflect the kingdom and the King. In other words, we are what we eat.[17]

For those of us who have felt left out of the kingdom's strategy and action by the parables of the mustard seed and the leaven, can there be a greater consolation and excitement? God has not just chosen to describe, identify and point out his kingdom to us. He has invested it inside of us, placing it at the very centre of our beings. We are not only pilgrims searching for the kingdom; we are subjects who have become the very dwelling place for the King. Everything that we have heard about the kingdom: its growth, its power, its eternal proportions, its battles, its victories, its certainties and its perfections, presents new possibilities for our own existence. All that we have seen God doing in creation and history can also happen in and through us. We have inherited the kingdom.

The question is, what will we do with such a marvellous birthright? How obvious is our inherited wealth to the world in which we live? When we go to work or spend time in our communities, do people see the kingdom in us? Do they see the upside-down world where there is good news for the poor, sight to the blind and freedom for anyone who would ask? Do they see the growth of the mustard seed as we live out extraordinary lives, for which the only explanation can be the internal reality of God's rule? Do they see the power of leaven as our lives fill the gaps of others and our actions lift the hearts of all who we meet through the power of the resurrection? Can people see that in us the kingdom has come and God's will is being done? Do they look at what we have and offer to sell everything they own for a slice of this kingdom?

THINGS TO DO

Martin Luther encourages us to think about our own part in this parable. He points out that the kingdom of God is hidden in the world because it is hidden in Christians who live in the world. As we live out the gospel in our everyday lives, the yeast of the kingdom penetrates the whole of society.[18]

Take some time to consider all the ways in which God has brought his perfect rule and order into your life. Reflect on the times in which the kingdom has found you, no matter how far you were away from the kingdom. Thank God that he didn't need a travel guide to get to you.

NOTES FROM FELLOW TRAVELLERS

'The kingdom of God comes of itself, without our prayer, but we pray in this petition that it may also come to us.'

Martin Luther

'Faithfulness is not just living with the inevitable; it is living in a God-context where we are able to see what he is doing and join him in the middle of it.'

Viv Thomas[19]

PLACES TO GO

The kingdom of God is within you – Luke 17:20-21
The kingdom of God is coming – Luke 9:1
We're on the invite list – Luke 10:19-20

PLACES TO STAY

'I bind unto myself today the power of God to hold and lead, his eye to watch, his might to stay, his ear to hearken to my need, the wisdom of my God to teach, his hand to guide, his shield to ward, the Word of God to give me speech, his heavenly host to be my guard.'

Fourth century Celtic prayer attributed to St Patrick[20]

KINGDOM SIGHTINGS

Brother Andrew is famous in the Christian world under another title: God's Smuggler. This Dutch-born Christian dedicated his life to smuggling Bibles into Communist countries, and has an amazing story to tell of God's kingdom manifesting itself in his life. Brother

Andrew lived a life of adventure, action and service. But he is always very clear on the absolute sovereignty of God, and on how his role was nothing more than one of obedience to the king.

'If I were going to give my life as a servant to the king, I had to know that king. What was he like? In what way could I trust him? In the same way I trusted a set of impersonal laws? Or could I trust him as a living leader, as a very present commander in battle? The question was central. Because if he were a king in name only... I would remain a Christian, but I would know that my religion was only a set of principles, excellent and to be followed, but hardly demanding devotion.

'Suppose on the other hand that I were to discover God to be a person, in the sense that he communicated and cared and loved and led. That was something quite different. That was the kind of king I could follow into any battle.'

Brother Andrew[21]

- -

TOUR GUIDE

It is difficult, if not impossible, for a twenty-first century person living in a republic, a federation, or even a constitutional monarchy to really understand what is meant when God is called 'King.' There was a very definite link in ancient times between kingship and divinity, and even today there are nations where the king is considered a god, and is accorded religious worship. In Europe the best and most recent example of this link can be found in the absolute monarchs of the 17th and 18th centuries, in particular Louis XIV of France. These monarchs were not considered divine themselves, but they claimed to have been given the 'Divine Right of kings' by God, and thus felt justified in exercising a kind of autocratic, infallible rule in their nations. According to historian J. M. Roberts, 'under Louis XIV, absolute government reached its climax in France and became a model for all European princes... the French church's independence from Roman authority was asserted, but only to bring it more securely under the wing of the monarchy... it was the triumph of hierarchical, corporate, theocratic society.[22]

Louis XIV's power in France was total. He was ultimately responsible for everything, and everyone was ultimately responsible to him. There could be no thought of anyone else acting on behalf of France unless it was expressly approved by the king himself. These representatives would then not be acting on their own authority, but on authority derived from the king. No other political force was permitted; the role of everyone else was to administer the king's policies. This type of sovereign power was perhaps best summed up by Louis XIV in his famous pronouncement 'L'état, c'est moi,' – 'I am the state.'

While it would be most incongruous to compare Louis XIV's egotistical tyranny to the reign of the King of all Kings, it must be pointed out that God is the one true absolute monarch. No one in the kingdom can act on their own authority; any authority we have has been given to us by the King (Lk. 9:1, 10:19-20). It is entirely appropriate for God to say: 'I am the kingdom.'

THINGS TO DO

→ Try breaking your personal best gospelling record. See how many random acts of good news you can punctuate your day with. Take time during the day to be good news to the people around you. Kingdom warning! You may find that such behaviour is strangely addictive and generates many an unusual response.

→ Take time to pray Steve Turner's *Psalm*:

Not my works
But your work
Not my perfection
But yours
Not my grasp
But your grip
Not my completeness
But yours.

Not my strength
But your strength
Not my honesty
But yours
Not my trust
But your truth
Not my will be done
But yours.

Steve Turner[23]

USEFUL WORDS AND PHRASES

'Jesus went throughout Galilee, preaching the good news of the kingdom' (Mt. 4:23). As I write this I find myself with my in-laws in South Africa. Today, on three separate occasions, the fluent second language of my family has been interrupted with the following notion;

'You know that word doesn't really translate into English.' Now it is my turn to point out that some things just don't translate. George Eldon Ladd suggests a better translation of this verse would read: 'Jesus was gospelling the kingdom of God all over the place.' For Jesus the good news of the kingdom was not so much a sermon to be preached as a life to be lived. His whole being was the bringing of good news. It was this totality of goodness that caught his disciples' attention and became their obsession. So much so that in his absence they began gospelling too (Acts 8:12). Let's follow the example of Jesus. Let's stop waiting for opportunities to preach to those who'll listen and let's start gospelling the good news of the kingdom to everyone we meet.[24]

- -

[1] B. H. Young, *The parables, Jewish tradition and Christian interpretation* (Massachussetts: Hendrickson Publishers Inc., 1998)

[2] C. Baird, from the song *We're in God's army and we fight* published in *The Songbook of the Salvation Army* (London: Salvationist publishing and supplies, 1986) Song 705

[3] E. Booth, from the song *The world for God* published in *The Songbook of the Salvation Army* (London: Salvationist publishing and supplies, 1986) Song 830

[4] A. J. Hultgren, *The parables of Jesus: a commentary* (Grand Rapids: W. B. Eerdmans Publishing Co., 2000) pp389-390

[5] R. H. Gundry, *Matthew: a commentary on his handbook for a mixed church under persecution* (Grand Rapids: W. B. Eerdmans Publishing Co., 1994) p267

[6] Henri Nouwen, *With open hands*, quoted in *Seeds of hope: a Henri Nouwen reader*, edited Robert Durback (Toronto: Bantam Books, 1989) pxvii

[7] E. Peterson, *Praying with Jesus* (San Francisco: Harper, 1993)

[8] Tony Campolo, *The kingdom of God is a party* (Dallas: Word Publishing, 1990) p39

[9] R. T. France, *New Testament profiles: Matthew, evangelist and teacher* (Illinois: InterVarsityPress, 1989) pp144-146

[10] R. H. Gundry, *Matthew: a commentary on his handbook for a mixed church under persecution* (Grand Rapids: W. B. Eerdmans Publishing Co., 1994) p268

[11] Pope John Paul ll, *Crossing the threshold of hope* translated by Jenny and Martha McPhee, edited Vittorio Messori (London: Jonathan Cape, 1994) p38

[12] Douglas Coupland, *Life after God* (Toronto: Pocket Books, 1994)

[13] M. Ouaknin, *Symbols of Judaism* (New York: Assouline, 2000) p14

[14] Paraphrased from Bart Campolo, *Kingdom Works* (Michigan: Servant Publications, 2001) p139

[15] *The Shawshank Redemption* (Cinema Club 1997)

[16] D. Kraybill, *The upsidedown kingdom* (Scottdale: Herald Press, 1990)

[17] T. F. Torrance, *Kingdom and the Church: a study in the theology of the Reformation* (Eugene: Wipf and Stock Publishers, 1996) p81

[18] Martin Luther, *Weimarer Augsgabe of Luther's works* (Wein: 1883) p107

[19] Viv Thomas, *Future leader: spirituality, mentors, context and style for leaders of the future* (Carlisle: Paternoster Press 1999) p136

[20] St. Patrick, quoted in Viv Thomas, *Future leader: spirituality, mentors, context and style for leaders of the future* (Carlisle: Paternoster Press 1999) p51

[21] Brother Andrew with John and Elizabeth Sherrill, *God's smuggler* (London: Hodder and Stoughton, 1967) pp73-74

[22] J. M. Roberts, *The Penguin history of the world* (Toronto: Penguin Publishing, 1990) pp553-554

[23] Steve Turner, *The king of twist* (London: Hodder and Stoughton, 1992) p90 (© Steve Turner. Reprinted by permission of the author and the Lisa Eveleigh Literary Agency)

[24] G. E. Ladd, *The gospel of the kingdom: scriptural studies in the kingdom of God* (Grand Rapids: W. B. Eerdmans Publishing Co., 1959) p126

CHAPTER 5

KINGDOM ECONOMY

The Parables of the Hidden Treasure and the Pearl –
Matthew 13:44-46

Economics is not my strong point, as a brief glance at my meagre bank balance will tell you. In spite of this, I was once asked to help lead a seminar on family finances, the aim being, I think, for me to give a 'youth' perspective on how to handle money. I began my talk by admitting that I was not sure why I had been asked to speak on the subject of economics, as it was not my area of expertise. As soon as I said that, a gentleman stormed out of the seminar. He would later compose a nasty note explaining how he had not paid to come and listen to someone who did not know what he was talking about.

Fair enough, I suppose. Economics is an important and intricate matter, and one which significantly affects our daily lives. It is also a major issue for a kingdom. One of the best ways for a traveller to understand a place he is visiting is to examine the financial practices of its citizens. What do they spend their money on? What do they consider to be necessities and priorities, as opposed to luxuries or a waste of money? And then, of course, the traveller must consider the fiscal policy of the kingdom itself. How does it budget its resources? What does it value? What is the standard for its money: gold? the US dollar? the Euro? Or something else entirely, something new and more precious than we could possibly comprehend?

Yes, economics is a complex and consequential subject. Fortunately, it is the parables of Jesus that will be leading you through on this part of your journey, and not me. Jesus is the master of the kingdom economy, and, well, economics is not my area of expertise...

5.1 Hide and Seek

> *LOCATION: 'The kingdom of heaven is like treasure hidden in a field. When a man found it, he hid it again, and then in his joy went and sold all he had and bought that field' (Mt. 13:44).*

I arrived at a friend's house recently to discover that he had disappeared. All I could hear were the delighted shrieks of his children playing. I followed this audible joy into the garden where, anxious not to interrupt, I became a spectator of a game of hide and seek. What immediately struck me was the way in which my friend played the game. Twice as high and almost twice as wide as his two young children, he continually hid himself in the most visible places. No matter where he hid there was always a protruding limb or some other unmistakable signpost to aid his children's discovery. To his kids, each find felt like the climax of a shrewd search or a complete accident. To me it was more obvious. Their father wanted them to find him.

This kingdom travel guide, whether we refer to this book or to the parables themselves, is in danger of turning into a very frustrating game of hide and seek. With each successive parable the kingdom seems to become more elusive. With each consecutive story, the kingdom seems to further resist explicit identification. If it has unsettled you as much as it is has me then you are probably at your wits' end. After all, a game of hide and seek is only exciting if there is a chance of the seeking turning into finding. Searching without the prospect of locating is as frustrating as it is pointless. So when will the hiding and seeking become finding and rejoicing?

D.W. Gooding has suggested that Matthew chapter 13 should be called 'Tactics for establishing the kingdom.'[1] At last, it may seem, we are on the verge of an exciting new discovery. 'The kingdom of Heaven is like treasure hidden in a field' (Mt. 13:44). Once again, we are back on the farm. Hiding treasure in the ground is an age-old method of storage and protection. By the first century, the inhabitants of Palestine have become quite accustomed to invasions from nearby kings and countries. These unwelcome visitors have a habit of plundering the property and

possessions of the Jewish people. In an attempt to protect their possessions and confound their enemies, many Jews take to depositing their
most valuable possessions in the ground beneath their feet. As a result,
it is not uncommon for people to discover buried treasure by all kinds of
means. In some instances a serendipitous find is considered to be a
reward for faithfulness and righteousness.[2] In other circumstances the
method of discovery is a lot less honourable. The Roman historian Josephus
records occasions when Roman soldiers would interrogate Jewish land-
owners to discover and loot these ancient safety deposit boxes.[3]

Fortunately, the hero of our present parable is no Roman soldier. He is
a labourer. Brad Young has suggested that he represents the ordinary
guy who is about to give up. Jesus seems to suggest that he wasn't even
looking for treasure, but that having dug some up, he cannot believe his
eyes. What great act or service could God be rewarding him for? Why had
all his birthdays arrived at once? Regardless of the answer, he has a problem to solve. Under the law, the treasure belongs to the owner whose
land it is buried in. As a farm-hand, this man could not have afforded to
buy this piece of ground without a considerable sacrifice. With this in
mind, he is forced to sell everything that he has and use the proceeds to
capture the land and thus the treasure buried within.

While travelling through the parable of the leaven, we asked the question: 'Why has God hidden the kingdom?' In our journey through this
parable, the question arises again. Is it because the kingdom treasure is
too priceless, too precious and too mysterious for it to be on open
display? That may be a partial answer. But the story also tells us that God
has hidden the kingdom because he wants it to be found. He is the King
who loves to play hide and seek, but to be honest, by our standards he is
not very good. He is the Father who is always anxious for his children to
find him when they come looking.

This is the irony of these parables. On the one hand, they stand as
evidence for the elusive mysteries of the kingdom. On the other, they
form a treasure map which leads us straight to the buried treasure that
we have, or even haven't, been looking for. In these parables, as in life
itself, the kingdom is both hidden and found. While it may have been
beyond our discovery in the past, it is now in our grasp for the future.
Jesus has told us where it is; he himself is the X that marks the spot.

Whenever we find him, we find the King and the kingdom. His Holiness John Paul II affirmed this, saying: 'It is precisely in [his] birth, and then through the Passion, the Cross, and the Resurrection that the self-revelation of God in the history of man reached its zenith — the revelation of the invisible God in the visible humanity of Christ.'[4]

Back to my friend's garden: having left his somewhat conspicuous cover, my friend greeted me and informed his kids that the game was over. Suddenly the joy seemed to drain from their whole afternoon. 'Please Dad, just one more game?' came their whining invocation. By now Dad had become a little bored, but his kids were still raring to go. It occurred to me that no matter how many times Dad went into hiding, they would come seeking. Each successful find seemed to propel them closer to delirium. For these children, the two best finds were always the last one and the next one.

NOTES FROM FELLOW TRAVELLERS

'Let's try to be impartial in our reasoning: Could God go further in His stooping down, in His drawing near to man, thereby expanding the possibilities of our knowing Him? In truth, it seems that He has gone as far as possible. He could not go further. In a certain sense God has gone too far! Didn't Christ become "a stumbling block to Jews and foolishness to Gentiles" (1 Cor. 1:23)? Precisely because He called God His Father, because He revealed Him so openly in Himself, He could not but elicit the impression that it was too much... Man was no longer able to tolerate such closeness, and thus the protests began.'

John Paul II[5]

'God will be the reward of virtue, who bestowed the virtue and gave the promise of himself, than whom nothing could be better or greater. What else did he mean when he spoke by the prophet "I will be their God and they shall be my people," but "I will be their satisfaction: I will be whatever men can honestly desire; life, health, food, wealth, glory, honour, peace, and every good thing"? That is the true meaning of the Apostle's words, "That God may be all in all." He will be the goal of our desires, whom we shall see for ever, whom we shall love without satiety and praise without weariness. This shall be the gift, the affection, the business of all, as life eternal shall be itself the common lot of all.'

St Augustine[6]

THINGS TO DO

When was the last time you caught a glimpse of the kingdom? What led you there? How did you respond? What did you do with the experience? Take some time to think about where you might expect to see the kingdom next. How intently are you looking for it? How excited are you by the prospect of finding it? What would you give up to possess it?

PLACES TO STAY

Listen to the song *I still haven't found what I'm looking for* by U2.[7]

KINGDOM SIGHTINGS

'I seek an Inheritance, incorruptible, undefiled, and that fadeth not away; and it is laid up in Heaven, and fast there, to be bestowed at the time appointed on them that diligently seek it.'[8]

John Bunyan's *The Pilgrim's Progress* is an allegorical account of the Christian journey of faith into the kingdom of God. In it we have the story of a man, named Christian, who undertakes a long and perilous quest. His goal is to escape the City of Destruction, where he and his family had been living, and to reach the Celestial City of the King. During the course of this travel he encounters many pitfalls, and many travelling companions; some helpful, some not. After many miles, captures, waylayings, beatings and battles, Christian finally makes it to his destination, the City of the King, where he is welcomed and where he finds his peace. All throughout his arduous adventures, Christian is buoyed up by a sustaining faith and hope in a city he has never seen. This is his description of the city of his dreams:

There is an endless Kingdom to be inhabited, and everlasting life to be given us, that we may inhabit that Kingdom forever... There are Crowns of Glory to be given us, and Garments that will make us shine like the Sun in the Firmament of Heaven...There shall be no more crying, nor sorrow; for he that is the owner of that place, will wipe all tears from our eyes... There we shall be with Seraphims, and Cherubims, creatures that will dazzle your eyes to look on them. There also you shall meet with thousands, and ten thousands that have gone before us to that place; none of them are hurtful, but loving, and holy. Everyone walking in the sight of God, and standing in his presence with acceptance forever.

John Bunyan[9]

Paul considers all else to be 'rubbish' in comparison with the knowledge of Christ – Philippians 3:7-11.

5.2 In or Out?

LOCATION: Matthew 13:44 (same as above).

The parables of the kingdom take their place in time and yet remain perfectly timeless. These stories transcend any traditional tense. These are not wistful tales of fancy or considerations of what could be if we are so lucky. As sure as history is history, the kingdom has come. But the kingdom cannot be limited to one conjugation. While the kingdom is in the past, it is not stuck in the past tense. These are stories about the present. They are taking place in our towns and streets as we write. More than this, they are stories about the future and they are coming to a situation near you. The kingdom has come but it certainly has not gone. It is still there to be found. It is still hidden only to be dug up, and while finding it once is to know joy unlimited, the search doesn't need to end there. This Father gives his children an unlimited amount of turns to find his unlimited treasure. When they discover it, the new joy is piled on top of the old. Time and time again, the kingdom has a limitless capacity for joy, surprise and discovery.

As the kingdom is not limited by time, neither is it limited by space. In other words, the kingdom cannot be confined to a building that we make a sacred pilgrimage to on a weekly basis. As the man finds the treasure in the field, we will find the treasure in the world, for that is what the field represents. This interpretation stands as a rebuke to those of us who go searching every Sunday for a kingdom removed from the world. The parable of the treasure is a big, red stop sign to people like me who get it into their unenlightened heads that the kingdom is only to be found in the lyrics of hymns and songs, the texts of sermons, the flowery prose of prayers and the Sabbath retreat from worldly people and earthly reality.

If there is such a kingdom to be found in our services and celebrations, it is not the one that Jesus is speaking about. The king who would only hide his kingdom under the vaulted roofs of churches and chapels is not the kind of king who is interested in being found. Jesus' stories do not take place in the inner courts of the Temple where only the holiest of the holy can enter. His hiding place is not a secret kept from the godless for the sake of the good. Jesus has made it quite clear that if this was the case, then only God could find the kingdom, because no one is good save him alone.

Unfortunately, throughout history the church has often fallen into the trap of thinking that she is synonymous with the kingdom. Pre-Reformation theology contained a certain arrogant strain which suggested the kingdom was little more than an ingredient of the church: 'where the church is, there is the kingdom also.'[10] For Luther, this presented a particular problem. If the church was the kingdom of God on earth, then does that mean that the kingdom of God is responsible for ecclesiastical mistakes? Furthermore, if the kingdom of God was limited to the realm of the church, what does this mean for every person and every place outside the church's reach? Were they beyond God's reach and power? In attempting to answer these types of questions, John Calvin eventually came to the conclusion that the kingdom had to be much bigger than the church. God's kingdom was not simply part of the church; rather, the church was part of God's kingdom.

The church and the kingdom are not identical; God has a greater and more certain reality in store than the one we see in the church. It is possible, though difficult, to mark out the boundaries of the church in this world. The actual limits of the kingdom in this world, suggests St Augustine, are known only to God himself.[11] The church is, of course, one of the key instruments used by God in his kingdom, but it is not the only one. Therefore, the kingdom must be present both inside and outside of the church's borders, and must be able both to encourage and disturb the church. Above all else, we must remember that the kingdom is everywhere that God is. And since God is omnipresent, so too is the kingdom.

It would of course be very wrong, and quite dishonest, for me to suggest that we can never find the kingdom in the church. I have often discovered the treasure of the kingdom in the life and community of the church. The church is full of kingdom theology, kingdom ideals, kingdom moments and kingdom communities. I have experienced the kingdom in songs, sermons, sacraments and salvations. It has been present in many moments and in real relationships. I could not even begin to count the kingdom treasure that I have discovered, intentionally and unintentionally, in the church. Similarly, I have discovered the kingdom in some of the most unexpected places outside of the church. I can remember many films and concerts, sights and conversations where I have been overcome by the beauty and magnificence of God's rule and order. However, the discoveries that spring to mind most readily are the ones which took place in both spheres at the same time.

In 1991, I travelled beyond the fallen Iron Curtain to witness the Salvation Army's work in the city of St Petersburg. Here, in a country recovering from enforced atheism, I saw the kingdom in a whole new way. I remember sitting and listening to the stories of a recently converted Russian poet. As he spoke of the anti-God propaganda that littered his childhood he confessed, 'Of course we all believed in God. We knew he must exist and we knew he must be powerful. Why would our leaders fear him so much otherwise?' As I discovered the kingdom of God in new ways outside the church, so too I discovered him in new ways inside the church. The missionaries whom we worked with had a different kind of order to their lives. Their priorities and their privileges were not the same as mine. They had discovered a treasure that was worth more than everything else that they owned or possessed. They gladly gave up careers and comfort for the treasure of the kingdom. They were prepared to travel to the other side of the world, away from their warm and welcoming churches, to dig up something so precious yet so uncertain. In their church and their world, the kingdom came to me. In a nation seemingly so devoid of God, God became more real than ever.

These vivid sightseeing tours of the kingdom have continued throughout my ministry. Whenever I see the church in the world, I see the kingdom clearly and feel that my faith is more authentic. I have dug up the kingdom while living in North America's poorest postal code, experiencing community with homeless people, addicts, prostitutes, and those suffering with HIV/AIDS. Seeing the kingdom powerfully and continually at work in this environment has taught me what salvation is really all about. I have also stumbled across the kingdom in South Africa, in Toronto, in Rostov on Don, in London and a hundred other places where I saw need and hope in equal extremes. In each of these visits, I saw that God births his kingdom into this world in us, around us, through us, and even without us. It is here that I have felt most alive to the presence and possibilities of the kingdom. At times like these I feel like a prince and heir to a royal kingdom. In moments like these I have experienced life eternal. In situations like these I realise that the people of the kingdom are the richest people on earth.

Jesus' kingdom can be found scattered around the whole field of humanity. This King has hidden the treasure of his kingdom under the ground on which all of us walk. Wherever we go the kingdom waits for us to trip over it, discover it, grasp it and keep it. It is in our work places, our streets and our communities. It waits for us on distant shores and lurks under every pavement. It is in our friendships and our friends. And yes, it is in our churches and our fellowships as they are all part of our world, no matter how hard they sometimes try not to be.

If we wish to buy the kingdom, whether as the church or as Christians, we must first buy the field. To gain the kingdom we must buy into the whole of creation. To discover the kingdom we must become part of God's plan for the whole planet, for that is what it means to be part of the church. We must be prepared to see the whole planet as part of God's kingdom. We must be prepared to scour the whole earth for the treasure of the kingdom. Remember, it is a kingdom that is working hard to be found.

NOTES FROM FELLOW TRAVELLERS

'Don't turn the church into a sodality that consists only of bright, white Anglo-Saxons who are happily married, have 1.8 children and never get drunk. Instead, just let it be what it in fact already is: a random sampling of the broken, sinful, half-cocked world that God in Christ loves – dampened by the waters of baptism but in no way necessarily turned into perfect peaches by them.'

R. F. Capon[12]

'This is what eternal life means. This is what it means to be saved. It means to go about every day in the present evil age living the life of heaven. It means that every local fellowship of God's people who have shared this life should live together and worship and serve together as those who enjoy a foretaste of heaven here on earth.'

G. E. Ladd[13]

KINGDOM SIGHTINGS

Mike Oshiro, a friend of mine, told me this story:

We were having a typical youth group outing, down at the beach. We had brought along a frisbee, some marshmallows, a football, and we were experiencing the joy of being young, crazy Christians on sand. Our fun was rudely interrupted, however, when we noticed a dirty, smelly, obviously drunk man closing in on our group. We had just begun playing some kind of hugging game, conceived no doubt by us boys in a desperate attempt to get some justified, sanctified, physical contact with the girls. So this man broke into our group, spread his arms wide apart, and spluttered:

'How's about a big hug for me?!'

There was no way I was hugging this man. And there was no way I was letting the girls hug this man, not that they were exactly getting in line to do so. I was one part nervous, two parts annoyed with this guy. He had disturbed our time of Christian fellowship, and was clearly just making fun of us by asking for a hug. I was considering being brave and asking this man to leave us alone.

But then one of the male members of the youth group did a remarkable thing. He walked over to the man, who still had his arms outstretched, and hugged him. And I mean, *really* hugged him. The drunken man was shocked; we were all shocked. Nobody said a word. And then slowly, the man put his arms around my youth group friend. They just stood there, on the beach, hugging like madmen. My friend told us that it was OK, we could leave them for a while. So we did leave, in a much more subdued and thoughtful manner.

We remained at the beach, but the whole time we were there my friend stayed with the man. Eventually, they went over to a bench, the man put his head down on my friend's lap, and my friend patted his head until he fell asleep. I simply could not understand why my friend had done this; it never even came near to entering my head to act in such a way. But my friend explained, 'This man probably has not been hugged, or even really touched, in years. He's had no human contact, and when he was joking around, asking for a hug, I could sense a real, desperate, human need. We're down here as part of a church youth group. I felt I had to respond to that cry for contact.'

Here is a true example of the kingdom of God existing where the church meets the world.

'Prayer does not demand that we interrupt our work, but that we continue working as if it were a prayer. It is not necessary to always be meditating, nor to consciously experience the sensation that we are talking to God, no matter how nice this would be. What matters is being with him, living in him, in his will. To love with a pure heart, to love everybody, especially to love the poor, is a twenty-four-hour prayer.'

Mother Teresa[14]

To seek for the kingdom is to crave nothing else but God, to consider everything else as absolutely worthless. This is the kingdom economy. God is worth everything; everything else is filthy rags. Justice, holiness, righteousness, peace – none of these things are the goal. God alone is the goal. These other things will come – God promises this – but not necessarily in the way we expect or understand. They will come in the way God wants them to come, and this is far better. To seek exclusively for the King is the way to the kingdom and everything else that comes with it.

THINGS TO DO

Start a new prayer strategy for at least one day. Instead of setting aside one portion of the day for God, set aside the entire day. Go about your day as per usual, but for each new activity you begin, no matter how mundane or 'non-spiritual', take a moment to say out loud or in your head: 'God, help me to worship you with this activity.' This is what Brother Lawrence describes as 'practising the presence of God.' As he puts it: 'I do nothing else but abide in his holy presence, and I do this by simple attentiveness and a habitual, loving turning of my eyes upon him. This I should call... a wordless and secret conversation between the soul and God which no longer ends.'[15] In this way you will begin to see how the kingdom cannot be contained within any structure or any time – it is everywhere you go.

PLACES TO GO

God created the earth, and it was good – Genesis 1
The renewal of all creation – Romans 8:18-25

5.3 Mother of Pearl! What a Deal!

 LOCATION: 'Again, the kingdom of heaven is like a merchant looking for fine pearls. When he found one of great value, he went away and sold everything he had and bought it' (Mt. 13:45-46).

If the labourer represents the ordinary guy on the street, the merchant represents the businessman in the market. The kingdom is there for anybody, whether rich or poor. What's more, the kingdom is there for those who discover it by accident and for those who give their life to the search. Jesus is clear that the merchant's pearl-hunt is both planned and ongoing. This is not a story about a man who has stumbled upon treasure by accident. This is a story about a man who has committed his life to the discovery of the finer things. This businessman knows his business, is well-informed about the market, is aware of the worth of his merchandise and is always looking to get ahead of the game. He can spot a bear or a bull from a long way off. He buys low and sells high. He is intent on making the deal.

The pursuit of the pearl is more than a piece of good business. The pearl is as precious a symbol as it is a commodity. The pearl is the beginning of adventure and the commencement of a quest. Ancient literature is filled with stories of brave heroes who travel the ends of the earth in the hope of discovery. This is the stuff of epic and romance. 'The discoverer must do all he can to obtain it [the pearl]. Part of the drama is the acquiring. In matters of the heart, pursuing the object of desire can be as splendid as the acquiring.'[16] The merchant searches for the pearl not only for what he can make of it, but for what it can make of him. To find such treasure would not only prove him shrewd and tenacious, but also noble and righteous. In the moment of discovery, what to everyone else is irrational becomes the only sane thing to do. In an instant his decision is made. His audit is complete. All else is worthless rubbish compared to such beauty. All else is joyless compared to such ecstasy. The merchant sells up and the adventure is fulfilled.

The merchant represents all of us who are desperate to find the kingdom: the travellers who will scour the maps of Jesus' life in travel guides like this book. The merchant is the man who plans his journey knowing that the treasure is out there, waiting and wanting to be found. The merchant stands for those of us who have tasted the kingdom, become hooked on it, and will go anywhere for another taste. Those like the missionaries I mentioned above, the ones who went to the end of the world, knowing nothing more than the kingdom they were looking for and the King they were following. The merchant symbolises every Christian who has braved the big bad world in an attempt to make a difference, whatever the cost. He finds his pearl on behalf of every traveller who lives in the hope that one day God would vindicate their efforts and their search with a moment of unbelievable discovery. Here, in the penultimate parable of the kingdom we meet the readers and the writers of this book — we see ourselves. As I write these words, and as you read them, we are both staring into a mirror, seeing the reflection of the merchant who is seeking desperately for his perfect pearl.

As we inject ourselves into the story as the protagonist, we should try to become more familiar with the main question it presents. Is the parable of the pearl about the value of the kingdom or the price of gaining it? Scholars have long played intellectual tennis with this question.[17] Having watched this game at close hand, mesmerised by the skill of the various contestants, I have come to the conclusion that both sides are winners. This may seem like a cop-out, but I'm sticking with it.

Of course this parable is about the value of the kingdom. The deal may prove costly from the merchant's point of view, but in real terms it is the bargain of a lifetime. When we consider his dilemma further, it simply disappears before our eyes. He gets the divine rule of God, the perfect and infinite justice of the Father, an eternal relationship with the King as Father, and the inheritance of all that belongs to the Lord of creation. In return he gives up his broken, sinful and temporary existence. This deal is what a businessman might call a 'no-brainer'. This kingdom is what one scholar has called 'sheer gift'.[18]

However, if Jesus considered it necessary to make mention of the enormous personal cost to the merchant in the story, then it must be important enough to gain our consideration. While what we own may be nothing compared to eternity, it is still everything to us. And the process of relativising our 'everything' into his 'nothing' is not that easy. It is especially hard for those of us who have grown used to having everything we want and everything we need, or at least everything we think we need. The merchant is not a labourer. Who knows how wealthy he is or how large his estate? Jesus does not inform us of how many pearls he has acquired to date or what risks and adventures were undertaken in their pursuit. What we do know is that he gave them all up, and there must have been some sorrow at their parting.

I'm pretty sure we still don't have an accurate appreciation of the cost of the kingdom. Perhaps a personal illustration, and another of Jesus' comments on the kingdom, may prove useful at this point. Over the last five years, my summers have become more and more reminiscent of Richard Curtis' wonderful film *Four Weddings and a Funeral*.[19] Before you worry too much about my moral well-being, let me explain. In the last five years, many of my friends have been busy falling in love and getting married. This has turned successive summers into a marvellous round of stag-nights, wedding ceremonies, dinners, discos and speeches. Having passed through this phase, I find myself looking for a sequel. While the weddings haven't dried up completely, the dedications, baptisms and christenings are occurring with a quickening speed and force. In a bid to understand my new identity and lifestyle I am hoping that Richard Curtis' next film will be about four christenings and a cremation.

My generation has begun its baby boom and everywhere you go there are booming babies. The moving and celebrative ceremonies of new life are often tainted for me by the recurrence of a certain Bible verse, one I have even seen depicted in stained glass on a baptismal font. In Matthew's gospel Jesus says, 'Let the little children come to me, and do not hinder them, for the kingdom of Heaven belongs to such as these' (Mt. 19:14). Part of me wonders whether Jesus ever regretted saying this, as it must have become one of the most misquoted and misused verses of Scripture, particularly when it comes to christenings and dedications.

Jesus' aligning of the kingdom with little children is not his apologetic for a simple faith. This is not Jesus letting his disciples off from the painful and bewildering complexities of what it means to follow him. This is not Jesus' manifesto for a world where theology and philosophy don't matter; there are plenty of better verses where Jesus makes thinkers into fools. No, as much as we would like it, this reference to children

isn't Jesus being cute or Jesus showing his interest in pre-school education. On the contrary, this is Jesus at his most brutal, his most honest and
most explicit. This statement is an invoice for all those who think they
can afford the kingdom.

It is hard for us to grasp what Jesus is saying here, as in the West the
wonder of youth and childhood has never been so protected. Successive governments, for all the right reasons, have chosen to create endless legislation as to how children and young people should be treated,
educated, nourished, housed, disciplined, nurtured, and so on. In first
century Palestine, the concept of child protection does not exist. Children have no rights. No child would stand in a court of law and give
testimony of the abuse they had suffered, for no child would be admit-
ted into a court of law. There is no legislation preventing excessive levels
of child labour or for the provision of education. The phrase 'human
rights' is simply untranslatable to one of these children. To this end,
Jesus selects the most vulnerable, the most misused and most abused
members of the population, and transforms them into the advert for
vacancies in the kingdom.

In this verse, Jesus gives one of his most terrifying estimates as to the
cost of kingdom membership. To become a member of the kingdom is to
become a child, simply to forgo all human rights. In the kingdom, your
only right is that of service and submission to the king. The phrases 'I
want', 'I need' and 'I deserve', are struck from your dictionary. To become
a member of the kingdom is to give up everything you own and everything
you are. To become a member of the kingdom is to realise that you deserve
nothing, but get everything.

When I read the parable of the pearl, I am struck by the price that the
merchant was willing to pay. When I look at my friends and heroes who
have given everything up for the kingdom, I am shaken by the sacrifices
they have made. The cost is unbelievable, but it is not the cost on which
they dwell. In fact, the price seems of little importance to the merchant
or to my friends. It is, in all seriousness, an irrelevance. For them there is
simply the treasure of the kingdom and joy unlimited. The unlimited joy
that it has brought them always far outweighs the price that was paid. I
know immediately that they are richer than me, for they know both the
value and the joy of the kingdom.

THE HITCHHIKER'S GUIDE TO THE KINGDOM

NOTES FROM FELLOW TRAVELLERS

'Indeed, how divided my heart has been and still is! I want to love God, but also to make a career. I want to be a good Christian, but also to have my successes as a teacher, preacher, or speaker. I want to be a saint, but also enjoy the sensations of the sinner. I want to be close to Christ but also popular and liked by many people. No wonder that living becomes a tiring enterprise. The characteristic of a saint is, to borrow Kierkegaard's words, "To will one thing." Well, I will more than one thing, am double-hearted, double-minded, and have very divided loyalty... "Set your hearts on His kingdom first... and all these things will be given you as well" (Mt. 6:33). You cannot follow Him just a little bit. Everything or nothing.'

Henri Nouwen[20]

'The Kingdom is infinitely beyond human value, but these parables teach that the Kingdom is within one's grasp if one is willing to sacrifice all to obtain it.'

B. H. Young[21]

The rich young man would not pay the price; the disciples would – Matthew 19:16-30

Whatever it takes – Philippians 3:7-11

Granny Weatherwax

Terry Pratchett has written a set of fantasy/comedy novels called the *Discworld* Series. They are extremely funny and thought-provoking, and well worth a read. In one of the books, entitled *Carpe Jugulum*, we read about Mr Oats, a young missionary of the Omnian religion – a faith which at one time was violently dogmatic, but which has fallen into extreme relativism and schism. Mr Oats is attempting to proselytise to a community of witches, vampires, werewolves and other assorted creatures. He meets with limited success. He has a particular struggle with the head witch, Granny Weatherwax. Mr Oats' faith is based on having witnessed the great incarnation of the god Om, when he appeared in the form of a small turtle to save his people. Granny Weatherwax has difficulty understanding how a faith that is based on such obvious divine intervention could become so watered-down. How could people who had seen such an incredible event, such a priceless treasure, not give their whole lives to this god? She delivers the following statement to Mr Oats, which seems also to serve as a statement by Terry Pratchett about the modern state of Christianity as he sees it:

Now if I'd seen him, really there, really alive, it'd be in me like a fever. If I thought there was some god who really did care two hoots about people, who watched 'em like a father and cared for 'em like a mother... well, you wouldn't catch me sayin' things like 'There are two sides to every question,' and 'We must respect other people's beliefs.' You wouldn't find me just being gen'rally nice in the hope that it'd all turn out right in the end, not if that flame was burning in me like an unforgivin' sword. And I did say burnin', Mister Oats, 'cos that's what it'd be. You say that you people don't burn folk and sacrifice people any more, but that's what true faith would mean, y'see? Sacrificin' your own life, one day at a time, to the flame, declarin' the truth of it, workin' for it, breathin' the soul of it. That's religion. Anything else is just... is just bein' nice. And a way of keepin' in touch with the neighbours.

Granny Weatherwax, in *Carpe Jugulum*[22]

Terry Pratchett, like Granny Weatherwax, seems to be confused as to why a people who claim to have knowledge of an incredible God don't think the worship of him is worth their whole lives.

'In 1929 I returned from Shanghai to my home town of Foochow. One day I was walking along the street with a stick, very weak and in broken health, and I met one of my old college professors. He took me into a teashop where we sat down. He looked at me from head to foot and from foot to head, and then he said: 'Now look here; during your college days we thought a good deal of you, and we had hopes that you would achieve something great. *Do you mean to tell me that this is what you are?*' Looking at me with such penetrating eyes, he asked that very pointed question. I must confess that, on hearing it, my first desire was to break down and weep. My career, my health, everything had gone, and here was my old professor who taught me law in the school, asking me: 'Are you still in this condition, with no success, no progress, nothing to show?'

But the very next moment – and I have to admit that in all my life it was the first time – I really knew what it meant to have the 'Spirit of glory' resting upon me. The thought of being able to pour out my whole life for my Lord flooded my soul with glory. Nothing short of the Spirit of glory was on me then. I could look up and without a reservation say, 'Lord, I praise Thee! This is the best thing possible; it is the right course that I have chosen!' To my professor it seemed a total waste to serve the Lord; but that is what the Gospel is for – to bring each of us to a true estimate of His worth.'

Watchman Nee[23]

THINGS TO DO

George MacDonald once wrote:

'You will not sleep, if you lie there a thousand years, until you have opened your hand and yielded that which is not yours to give or to withhold. You may think you are dead, but it will only be a dream; you may think you have come awake, but it will still be only a dream. Open your hand, and you will sleep indeed – then wake indeed.'

Take a moment to do this exercise:

Open up the palms of your hands, and imagine that your whole life is resting in them: your job, your family, your church, your finances, your friends, your concerns, your joys, everything that makes up 'you.' Feel the weight of it in your hands.

Now clench your fists very tight, almost to the point where it hurts. This symbolises our attitude to the things we think belong to us. We do not want to give them up.

Now, with your hands still in a tight fist, turn them over so that they are facing the ground. Imagine that God's hands are situated directly under yours, palms open. Try to picture what the palms of God look like.

When you are ready, open your fists, and watch your life – all the things that 'belong' to you – falling into the hands of God. Feel the weight of your life dropping away. Wipe your hands together, showing that you do not want to hold on to any part of your life.

Then turn your hands over again, with your palms facing up. Imagine God's hands directly above yours, waiting to drop *his* life, his kingdom into your hands. Feel the glorious weight of the kingdom of God in your hands, and close your fists tight again to show that you will hold on tight to this incredible gift.

Thank God for this incredible bargain he has offered to you.

If you have any difficulty releasing your life or aspects of your life into the hands of God, pray that God would enable you fully to sacrifice all that you have for the sake of his kingdom.

5.4 Joy of Man's Desiring

> *LOCATION: Matthew 13:44-46 (same as above).*

The price that we pay for the kingdom is overturned by the joy that comes with it. 'The word "joy" cannot be passed over lightly. Joy is an emotion that cannot be brought by one's plans, methods, or efforts. It is induced from factors outside the self. Unlike happiness, which people seek, joy can be present in a person's life even in times of pain and in moments when faith is tested severely.'[24] As if the kingdom was not enough we get this extra gift of joy on top. 'If we want to hear the ticking of Jesus' mind we can hardly do better than to study his parabolic words over and over — with our minds open not only to learning but to joy.[25]

In reading these parables, I have been convicted as to the lack of joy in my life and my church. Maybe there's something about being English which lowers my capacity for the abandonment that joy brings. This may be the result of years of bitter disappointment due to my nation's dismal record in meaningful sporting events. My mother tongue is the well-known dialect of English called Negativitese: 'How are you?' you ask. 'Not bad,' I say.

'How is work going?' you persist.

'Could be worse,' I reply.

'Would you like this piece of cake?'

'I wouldn't say no,' I respond.

I seem to get more negative and cynical by the day. My life apes the culture of the sarcastic sitcoms I watch. Is the joy of the kingdom at hand when I construct ten negative thoughts for every positive one?

C. S. Lewis once wrote, while considering the various Psalms of joyful abandonment, that most Christians seem to be missing out on this aspect of faith. He noted that his Anglican denomination was not noted for its joy, but suggested that other denominations, including the Roman Catholics, the Orthodox and the Salvation Army, had been more successful at holding on to theirs. Now, I cannot speak for the Catholic or Orthodox churches, but I do know that the Salvation Army, at least in the West, is no longer exactly living up to its former reputation for the rapturous

celebration of the living God. We have, in many areas, replaced sponta-
neous joy with predictable, suppressing traditionalism.

It seems that much of the church in the West has followed this trend.
Our fellowships appear joyless, they repel rather than attract. There is
a great distrust in the 'traditional' churches of the 'charismatic' movement. We fear perhaps that if that kind of freedom of expression is given
a foothold we may lose all sense of reason and dignity. Eighty-six year old
female parishioners might start swinging from the chandeliers; burly youths
with long hair might start playing music that sounds like rock and/or roll.
Having been in many a buttoned-down church environment in my time, I
can assure you that this kind of unbridled enthusiasm is probably the
least of our worries. We are not in any immediate danger of being overcome with joyous abandonment. Quite the contrary, our world view is
largely negative, and we are always so much quicker to judge than we
are to affirm. Our news is often bad, the price of the kingdom is over-
played, and the joy hardly mentioned. For this reason, if the church is to
be a signpost marking the way to the kingdom then it will have to rediscover the meaning of joy.

Some might say that the church's position in the West makes joy
impossible. For those of us who have become used to declining numbers and diminishing influence, joy has become a stranger. But such a
response rejects two important aspects of the joy of the kingdom.
Firstly, this joy is not about our success, whether or not we are doing
well in the eyes of the world. This joy is not brought on by statistics or by
impressive shows of strength and fruitfulness. This joy is a part of the life
that the Creator has breathed into his people. As such it is not about
what we can do, or have done for God. Rather it is about what God has
done and is doing in and through us. Therefore, if this kind of unexplained joy is absent from our life as the church, we should not be blam-
ing the world. We should be looking to ourselves, and asking how we have
come to miss out on the treasure of the kingdom of God. The time may
have come to start another epic search, to go into the world and to risk
all once again for the hope of the kingdom.

The second aspect of kingdom joy that we have mistaken should be
striking us in the face every time we walk through these two parables.
The story of the treasure and the pearl presupposes that we disciples,

as the inheritors of the kingdom, have exactly what the world wants. We do not have to be insecure about the news we tell, the product we push or the person we promote. And yet, as Robert Farrah Capon has observed, 'We offer to sell them the mystery of the love of God in Jesus; but the way we talk about God and Jesus only makes it sound like we are trying to peddle a live rattlesnake.'[26] What we have is the logical and miraculous conclusion of all human searching and yearning. The kingdom has the answer to every question that our friends and communities have ever asked. There is nothing to be embarrassed about and everything to brag about. This is the kingdom economy, and joy is its currency.

PLACES TO STAY

'The password of the early Christians was joy, so let us still serve the Lord with joy. Joy is love, joy is prayer, joy is strength. God loves a person who gives joyfully, and if you give joyfully you always give more. A joyful heart is the result of a heart burning with love. Works of love are always works of joy. We don't need to look for happiness: if we have love for others we'll be given it. It is the gift of God.'

Mother Teresa[27]

NOTES FROM FELLOW TRAVELLERS

'People say that we must have quiet, proper, decorous services. I say, where is your authority for this?!'

Catherine Booth

TOUR GUIDE

Pearls – taken primarily from the Red Sea, the Persian Gulf and the Indian Ocean – were considered to be of very high value in ancient India, Mesopotamia, and Persia. They are thought to have been introduced to the Mediterranean world after the conquests of Alexander the Great in the Orient. They are mentioned in neither the literature of ancient Egypt prior to that time, nor the Old Testament. According to Pliny the Elder (first century AD) pearls were considered the most valuable of goods, having 'the first place' and 'topmost rank among all things of price.' Within the New Testament pearls are of great value, along with gold (1 Tim. 2:9) and precious stones (Rev. 17:4, 18:12-16). In some instances pearls were considered more valuable than gold.

A. J. Hultgren[28]

'The Torah was to the Rabbis the pearl of great price. It contained, as it were, the kingdom of God within itself. By studying and serving the Torah, by practising it and fulfilling its laws, the Israelite both accepted and took upon himself the glad yoke of the kingdom; he widened the range of the kingdom, and in the eschatological sense he brought the advent of the kingdom nearer.'   Brad Young[29]

An Orthodox Jew in first century Palestine would daily recite the Shema as a symbol of his willingness to sacrifice all for the surpassing joy and treasure of the kingdom.

THINGS TO DO

→ Hang out with children.

I live in a community of severe despair, poverty and hopelessness. It is not really a child-friendly environment, but every week I take a large group of children to a local park nicknamed 'Needle Park', which is a reflection on the number of drug users who call it home. Scattered around the park when we arrive are knots of drunk or 'high' individuals with vacant looks on their bruised faces. But those looks change when the kids come streaming in to play. There is a playground set aside for them, and a number of park users join together to keep it clean and safe for the children. As the children walk around the park, yelling 'God bless you!', or pretending to be seagulls, the spirit of joy invades this darkest of places. The children do not see the bad, they only see the good, and they celebrate the good things of God with every ounce of their energy. We have found that the joy of children is one of the most powerful weapons in our kingdom arsenal. So hang out with children, and learn the joy of the Lord from them.

→ Recite the Shema.

'Hear, O Israel: The Lord our God, the Lord is one. Love the Lord your God with all your heart and with all your soul and with all your strength. These commandments that I give you today are to be upon your hearts. Impress them upon your children. Talk about them when you sit at home and when you walk along the road, when you lie down and when you get up. Tie them as symbols on your hands and bind them on your foreheads. Write them on the door-frames of your houses and on your gates.' Deuteronomy 6:4-9

PLACES TO GO

A song of joy to the Lord for who he is and what he has done – Psalm 33:1-5.

Ceaseless worship

During the dark days of the Second World War a priest found himself incarcerated within a German prisoner-of-war camp. The starkly brutal regime was intolerant of the man's calling and even less inclined to grant him license. However, the confiscation of his Bible and prayer book were not enough to deter this man from his God-given work and worship. As he manoeuvred around the camp the minister conducted a subversive survey. With each inmate interviewed, the priest began to recruit the strangest scribes that you ever saw. Each willing volunteer took it upon himself to scribble out as many Bible texts as his tired memory would allow. With painstaking care, and much danger besides, the beleaguered inmates were transformed into monks and their tatty scraps of paper became illuminated with the stuff of divine revelation. However it was not long before their endeavours were interrupted. A loose tongue and a carelessly hidden piece of evidence had found them out and now vengeance was unleashed. The oppressive regime rounded on the ringleader and allotted him a fate, they thought, worse than death. New daily duties assigned, the persecuted priest was marched to the sewer. Pushing him into the teeming waste, the guards stood back overcome by the pungency of the fumes. The holy man waded knee deep to the outlet where, with his bare hands, he began his new career. His job was to sweep, and pull, and push, and stir, and mix all manner of blockages until the high pipe was clear. What kind of job was this for hands anointed to break bread? Not long after his first day on the job, the priest's hand passed over a strange and recognisable texture. He swung, and dug, and scraped around and pulled from the excrement a piece of pure parchment. Cleaning the scrap, he discovered a text in quite a familiar hand. Within minutes more, he found every other page of the partial scriptures that he and his brothers had so carefully copied. What divine intervention was this? From this day forth the priest spent all his days in a cesspit of praise. He read, and prayed, and sang, and shouted his heart inside out. What's more, no guard ever realised what his punishment had become. The priest's secret and ceaseless worship was drowned out by smell alone.

1   R. T. France, *New Testament profiles: Matthew, evangelist and teacher* (Illinois: InterVarsityPress, 1989) pp144-146

2   B. H. Young, *The parables, Jewish tradition and Christian interpretation* (Massachussetts: Hendrickson Publishers Inc., 1998) p213

3   B. H. Young, *The parables, Jewish tradition and Christian interpretation* (Massachussetts: Hendrickson Publishers Inc., 1998) p214

4   Pope John Paul ll, *Crossing the threshold of hope* translated by Jenny and Martha McPhee, edited Vittorio Messori (London: Jonathan Cape, 1994)

5   Pope John Paul ll, *Crossing the threshold of hope* translated by Jenny and Martha McPhee, edited Vittorio Messori (London: Jonathan Cape, 1994) pp40-41

6   St. Augustine, *The City of God*, abridged and translated by J. W. C. Wand (London: Oxford University Press, 1963) p412

7   U2, *The Joshua Tree* (Island Records, 1987)

8   J. Bunyan, *The Pilgrim's Progress*, edited by N. H. Keeble (Oxford: Oxford University Press, 1998) p14

9   J. Bunyan, *The Pilgrim's Progress*, edited by N. H. Keeble (Oxford: Oxford University Press, 1998) pp16-17

10 T. F. Torrance, *Kingdom and the Church: a study in the theology of the Reformation* (Eugene: Wipf and Stock Publishers, 1996) p2

11 St. Augustine, *The City of God*, abridged and translated by J. W. C. Wand (London: Oxford University Press, 1963) pxvii-xviii

12 R. F. Capon, *The parables of the kingdom* (Grand Rapids: W. B. Eerdmans Publishing Co., 1985) p137

13 G. E. Ladd, *The gospel of the kingdom: scriptural studies in the kingdom of God* (Grand Rapids: W. B. Eerdmans Publishing Co., 1959) p78

14 Mother Teresa, *Meditations from a simple path*, excerpted from *A simple path*, compiled by Lucinda Vardey (New York: Ballantine Books, 1996)

15 Brother Lawrence, *The practice of the presence of God* translated by E. M. Blaiklock (London: Hodder & Stoughton, 1999) p44

16 A. J. Hultgren, *The parables of Jesus: a commentary* (Grand Rapids: W. B. Eerdmans Publishing Co. 2000) p412

17 B. H. Young, *The parables, Jewish tradition and Christian interpretation* (Massachussetts: Hendrickson Publishers Inc., 1998) p220

18 A. J. Hultgren, *The parables of Jesus: a commentary* (Grand Rapids: W. B. Eerdmans Publishing Co., 2000) p413

19 *Four weddings and a funeral* (MGM, 1993)

20 Henri Nouwen, *With open hands*, quoted in *Seeds of hope: a Henri Nouwen reader*, edited Robert Durback (Toronto: Bantam Books, 1989)

21 B. H. Young, *The parables, Jewish tradition and Christian interpretation* (Massachussetts: Hendrickson Publishers Inc., 1998) p199

22 Terry Pratchett, *Carpe Jugulum* (San Francisco: Harper-Prism, 1999)

23 Watchman Nee, *The normal Christian life,* third and revised edition (Eastbourne: Kingsway Publications, 1961)

24 A. J. Hultgren, *The parables of Jesus: a commentary* (Grand Rapids: W. B. Eerdmans Publishing Co., 2000) p415

25 R. F. Capon, *The parables of the kingdom* (Grand Rapids: W. B. Eerdmans Publishing Co., 1985)

26 R. F. Capon, *The parables of the kingdom* (Grand Rapids: W. B. Eerdmans Publishing Co., 1985) p144

27 Mother Teresa, *Meditations from a simple path*, excerpted from *A simple path*, compiled by Lucinda Vardey (New York: Ballantine Books, 1996) p65

28 A. J. Hultgren, *The parables of Jesus: a commentary* (Grand Rapids: W. B. Eerdmans Publishing Co., 2000) pp419-420

29 B. H. Young, *The parables, Jewish tradition and Christian interpretation* (Massachussetts: Hendrickson Publishers, Inc., 1998) p211

CHAPTER 6

THE FUTURE OF THE KINGDOM

The Parable of the Net – Matthew 13:47-52

From period drama to sci-fi in a sentence: those of us who have been waiting for a dose of the kingdom's end times have had to wait a long time to get our fix. Up until now these stories have been rooted in the past, identified in the present, and only pointed towards the future. We've seen the history of the kingdom, and we have some idea how it is interacting with the everyday world, but we don't yet know where it's all heading. This is pretty important information for the traveller. When the final whistle blows, and the King ultimately and utterly establishes his kingdom, you'll want to know where it's safe to stand. You'll also want to be known as a true kingdom pilgrim and not just a nosy interloper.

In this last tale, Jesus wastes no time in the past tense before bypassing the present and giving his disciples a chance to look at the final scores. The parable of the dragnet follows a similar line to the parable of the weeds and picks out several themes which are both important to Jesus and to his biographer Matthew. Watch and see where the kingdom is going.

6.1 Dragnet

 LOCATION: 'Once again, the kingdom of heaven is like a net that was let down into the lake and caught all kinds of fish' (Mt. 13:47).

It is easy to forget that by the time Matthew got around to writing his gospel, the disciples have lived through all manner of momentous events. Not only do they see Jesus go to Jerusalem where he is tried and crucified, but they then come into repeated contact with their resurrected

Master. They are in attendance when Jesus ascends to heaven, licked with tongues of fire as he sends down his Spirit upon them, and moulded into the living body of Christ on the earth when Jesus breathes his very life into them. That's a pretty big couple of months for anyone.

By the time Matthew comes to write down the parables of Jesus, the infant church has become a spectacularly fast-growing, world-changing, mess-creating group of believers who are spread across many cities, cultures and countries. Amidst this wonderful, powerful chaos, the apostles are charged with the deposit of faith that God had given them, by his Spirit, for the leadership of the church. This responsibility brings all kinds of joys and frustrations to the apostles' agendas. Gundry suggests that among Matthew's prime concerns is the differentiation between true and false disciples.[1] In part this is why the kingdom parables in chapter 13 are so important to Matthew's story of Jesus' life. 'If this is what Jesus says the kingdom is like,' ponders Matthew 'then what should the kingdom citizens look like?' It is also why the last parable brings such a mixture of relief and fear: Jesus affirms that he knows his children when he sees them, but also lets us in on what will happen to those who do not have membership in his kingdom.

Jesus' story focuses on a dragnet. This simple fishing device took the form of a large weighted net. The dragnet would be thrown out from the shore or pulled from one boat to another. As the huge device was tugged along the bottom of the sea floor it would inevitably pick up everything in its wake. No fish, plant, or object would escape from its grasp.

Those who practice fishing as an art form with the perfect fly, bait, reel, rod and worm, might think the dragnet a rather brutal and unsophisticated technique. They'd be right, of course. However, the aim of this work was to put food on the table, as opposed to providing a pleasant leisure activity for a weekend away (if it is possible to consider spearing worms, gutting fish, and receiving unexpected and unsanitised hook-piercings a 'pleasant leisure activity.') The technique of the dragnet may have lacked artistry but it more than made up for it in pure product. The downside of the dragnet was that it made post-production much more complicated. The end result would have been a huge bulging net filled with good fish, bad fish and anything else that you would find in a Palestinian lake. Possibly even one of Jesus' old sandals.

Jesus intends for the metaphor of the dragnet to tell us some important truths about the coming of the kingdom itself. So powerful is God's present and oncoming rule that it literally draws everything in its wake. So insistent is God's future that nothing can avoid becoming part of it. So unrelenting is God's plan that all creation is wrapped up in it, both now and into the future. The kingdom dragnet leaves nothing behind. No form of life, not animal, vegetable or mineral, can escape its sweep. Which means that we must all be part of a movement called the kingdom of God. Whether we call ourselves Christians or not. Whether we believe or not. Whether we recognise it or not. We are all part of a universe which has been created by a magnificent and beautiful person called God. He has created because he wants to be known by his creation. He has patience with his creation because he loves it. He has worked in his creation because he has given himself to it. He is the beginning and the end. He started creation and he is finishing it as well.

So this is where the two cities or two kingdoms metaphor must inevitably break down. Even the kingdom of this world cannot escape the wide reaches of the kingdom of God. The journey from the 'City of Destruction' to the 'Celestial City' while it is in one sense long and difficult, is in another sense no journey at all. The kingdom of the world, and its governor, Satan, are not independent powers in their own right, and cannot exist apart from God's sustaining power. The opposition remains only because God allows it to, but he will not allow it forever. The King will invoke his royal authority in every inch of his creation, and no other regime will be recognised or tolerated. We are surrounded by the kingdom of heaven at all times. The real question is whether we want citizenship in this kingdom or not.

NOTES FROM FELLOW TRAVELLERS

'I am for certain informed that this our City [of Destruction] will be burned with fire from heaven, in which fearful overthrow, both myself, with thee, my wife, and you my sweet babes, shall miserably come to ruin; except (which, yet I see not) some way of escape can be found, whereby we may be delivered.'

John Bunyan[2]

'There is no separation between the "holy" and the "worldly", the "sacred" and the "secular". Life is one. God has embraced us in our woundedness and suffering. In acknowledging and accepting our suffering and that of others, there is great joy and cause for celebration. Nothing escapes God's grasp. There are grounds for hope.'

Jean Vanier[3]

The Singer is a narrative work by Calvin Miller, which uses the metaphor of a Singer to retell the story of Jesus' life and work. Jesus is the Singer, and he is set in opposition to the Devil, the World Hater.

'The Singer woke at midnight. In the stupor of half-consciousness – neither quite aware nor yet asleep – he was alone. The air was full of moans. With groans of grief and pity, the night was crying. He had never heard the darkness cry before.

'Where are you, World Hater?' he shouted.

'Standing in the doorway of the worlds – revelling in my melodies of ugliness and death.'

The Singer listened. The morbid air depressed him and he could not help but weep himself. He ached from the despair.

'How long have they cried beyond the doorway of the worlds?' he asked.

The World Hater seemed to summon up the volume of their moaning and then he shouted: 'They've moaned a million years – it never stops. They hurt with the pain that burns and eats the conscience – illuminating every failure. They never can be free. Crying is the only thing they know.'

'Poor souls! Have they nothing to look back upon with joy?' the Singer asked.

'No. Nor anything to look forward to with hope.'

'Could they never give up suffering for one small moment, every thousand years or so?'

'No. Never. They ache in simply knowing they will never cease to ache.'

'I'm coming to the Canyon of the Damned you know.'

'You dare not think that you could sing above their anguished dying that will never be dead.'

'You'll see, World Hater. I will come.'

'It's my domain!' the World Hater protested.

'You have no domain. How dare you think that you can hold some corner of the Earthmaker's universe and make it your own private horror chamber!'

'It is forever, Singer!'

'Yes, but not off-limits to the song. I'll smash the gates that hold the damned and every chain will fall away. I'll sing to every suffering cell of hate, the love song of my soul. I'll stand upon the torment of the Canyon of the Damned.'

The troubled air grew still. The World Hater stepped outside the universe – pulled shut the doorway of the worlds.

And Crying softly slept with Joy.

Calvin Miller[4]

PLACES TO GO

The great harvest of the earth – Revelation 14:14-20
Every knee shall bow, every tongue confess that Jesus is Lord –
Philippians 2:9-11
Our citizenship is in heaven – Philippians 3:20-21

PLACES TO STAY

Glorious things of thee are spoken,
Zion, city of our God;
He whose word cannot be broken
Formed thee for his own abode.
On the rock of ages founded,
What can shake thy sure repose?
With salvation's walls surrounded
Thou mayest smile at all thy foes.

Saviour, if of Zion's city
I through grace a member am,
Let the world deride or pity,
I will glory in the name.
Fading is the worldling's pleasure,
All his boasted pomp and show;
Solid joys and lasting treasure
None but Zion's children know.

John Newton[5]

THINGS TO DO

Map out your own journey to the Celestial City. Chart the major events and relationships in your life, and how they impacted you either towards or away from the City of God. Make sure to include the starting point of your journey, as well as any major detours or delays you encountered. You will not be able to complete the map of your

journey yet, but mark down where you think you are on your
pilgrimage.

USEFUL WORDS AND PHRASES

Imputatio – this word is used by Martin Luther to describe the tension
of the now and not yet of faith. The term holds together our present
justification through Christ's death and resurrection with the
acknowledgement that this has not yet taken full effect. 'We possess
Christ by faith and in the midst of our afflictions through hope we wait
for that righteousness which we possess already by faith.'[6] As a
result Christians are forced to live in two kingdoms, the kingdom of
God and the kingdom of this world.

6.2 Fried Fish

LOCATION: 'When it was full, the fishermen pulled it
up on the shore. Then they sat down and collected the
good fish in baskets, but threw the bad away. This is
how it will be at the end of the age. The angels will
come and separate the wicked from the righteous and
throw them into the fiery furnace, where there will be
weeping and gnashing of teeth' (Mt. 13:48-50).

A friend of mine was once asked whether he believed that all roads lead
to God. 'Yes,' he replied, 'on judgement day all roads will lead to God.' At
the end of the dragnet story, like at the end of the parable of the wheat
and weeds, we must face what seems to be a very harsh reality. Once
again, however, it is inappropriate to see the judgement of God as a
harsh reality. It is only ever fair to see this judgement as a just reality. If
we are to believe in a God of love we must also rejoice in a God of justice.
This is 'Operation Infinite Justice.' This is the God who can, somehow,
wrap up all of history in perfection.

All in all I find this subject, like much that we have discussed, beyond
my realm of capability. What I would say is that Jesus is quite clear about
who is the Judge of time and history. This job belongs to the one perfect
King who has overseen everything from the beginning. He will decide

which disciples are true, and which are false. He will make the necessary, just, and perfect reparations. I find this challenging as deep down
I believe that I would, and do, make a very good judge. I find it easy to
judge my fellow believers and my fellow man. What's more, I convince
myself that as a Christian, or a leader, or a theologian, I am qualified to
make those judgements. I find myself continually second-guessing the
Almighty by presuming that his ways are my ways and that my judgements
will be his. This parable convicts me deeply and assures me that perfect
justice can never be understood, let alone delivered, by someone as
fallen as myself.

This is not to say that God does not ask us to make decisions. As a team
leader and a church leader, I continually find myself having to make these
on issues of discipline, accountability, delegation and empowerment. All
of these require me to reach certain judgements about people, their
needs, their potential, their behaviour, etc, etc. In these situations what
I know of the kingdom is decisive in helping me to do the job that God has
given me. There is a big difference, however, between temporal judgements and absolute judgements. Only God can make decisions on the
latter. Only he can say whether someone is in or out of the kingdom. Only
God, thank God, can make the final judgement on someone's life. No
instant video replay needed here. The where, the how, the why, the
what, the when and the who of the kingdom all belong to God.

So once again, as before with the parable of the weeds, we have God
directing his angels to separate the righteous from the unrighteous, the
wheat from the weeds, the bad fish from the good. And once again the
unrighteous, this time the fish, have a one-way ticket into the fiery
furnace. I can't imagine this would be easy work. I once went fishing on
a pier overnight. We were fishing for sand trout and Spanish mackerel, or
so I was led to believe.

I am not a great fisherman, and I spent most of the time trying to stick
live, wriggling shrimps onto my hook, flailing my line into the water, slowly
reeling it back in, discovering that my bait had been stolen by criminal
denizens of the deep, and watching everyone else haul in loads of mon-
ster-sized, succulent fish. We were out there for a long time, and still I
had no joy in the catching department. The person who had accompa-
nied me on my fishing excursion had long since given up, and had gone

back to the car for a nap. But I was determined; I would not leave that pier without hooking a fish. My line was constantly getting snagged on seaweed and rocks, and it was a struggle to bring it back up to the surface. At one point I felt I had snagged a particularly nasty rock, and was really working to get free. I suddenly realised that the rock was fighting back. It was a fish! I reeled that line as hard as I could, and in my excitement to bring the fish up fast, I actually managed to impale it on the end of my rod.

So there I was, standing on the pier like a complete dunce, holding a long rod with a fish attached to the top like a smelly, writhing weathervane. I brought the rod and fish down to the ground, and thought very seriously about touching the still-squirming beast. It was gasping, and actually making a noise, sort of like a low, wet grunting, only somehow worse. It also very clearly had teeth. I was at a complete loss. Finally, a young girl came along, saw my predicament, and expertly removed the fish. She looked at it carefully and said: 'It's too small, no good; you won't want to keep it.' It would have been extremely difficult for me to have made that judgement by myself, having no frame of reference for the proper size or merits of fish. It took an expert to tell me whether or not the fish was a keeper. I did not want to throw the fish back, it was mine, I had caught it; it was very special to me. But it was the appropriate thing to do.

I would feel uncomfortable making the comparison between my silly fishing trip and the divine judgement at the end of the world, if Jesus hadn't said something very much like it already in the parable of the dragnet. Jesus is the expert judge, not us. And humans are far more precious to him than my fish was to me. He does not want to throw anyone back, but he has to be true to his nature, which is completely just. A good friend of mine likes to say to people, 'You know, if it was up to me, you'd be getting into heaven, and I probably wouldn't. I think you're a great person, and I know how sinful I am. But I'm not the judge, God is. And he knows way better than me.'

NOTES FROM FELLOW TRAVELLERS

'Grading, judging, deciding on relative merits – all that is very much part of the world's life. But we are not good at it – nobody is good at it.

Leave it to the angels. The parable emphasises the reality of
judgement, at the same time that it says we have no part in doing it.'

Eugene Peterson[7]

'Faith cannot stand otherwise than by looking to the coming of Christ.'

John Calvin[8]

PLACES TO GO

The fate of the residents of the two kingdoms – Luke 17:22-37

Be prepared – Luke 12:35-48

We cannot judge others, but we can be certain of our own salvation – 1
John 5:13

Let God judge – Romans 2:1-4

The judging of the sheep and the goats – Matthew 25:31-46

KINGDOM SIGHTINGS

Looking the part

I will never forget taking part in a weekend mission at this ultra-
traditional church which had one of the best youth outreaches I have
ever seen. We were there to support the volunteer youth worker, a
middle-aged, completely un-hip mother of two, who had been
successfully evangelising to non-churched youth in her community
for fifteen years.

The first night we were at the church, well over a hundred young
people showed up, the majority of whom were 'clubkids' – teenagers
who live for the fun of clubs, music, and usually the attendant
pleasures of drugs, alcohol and sex. So this youth worker had us run a
club that night, complete with loud music, lights, smoke, dancing
(gasp!), and a very short, very high-energy devotional. Not exactly
your typical church youth group pizza night. But to be honest, the
teens didn't come because of our little mission team, or even
because we put on a good club; they came because of the love and
trust they had for someone who unconditionally loved them and who
was actually living out what she believed. Teenagers can spot
hypocrisy over a mile away.

These club kids ended up hanging out with us for the whole
weekend, following us around as we did street evangelism, shooting
pool with us, and even coming to the Sunday morning and evening
services. It served as quite a visual contrast. The first twenty pews
were filled with neatly pressed suits, white gloves, and frilly hats; the
last pew was filled with nose rings, pink hair, baggy pants and Marilyn
Manson T-shirts. At the end of the evening service, there was a
challenge to accept Christ which, one assumed, was aimed pretty

directly into the back pew. Three people did become Christians that night: two of the club kids, and the senior lay leader in the church.

By any human measuring stick, this man would have been the perfect Christian. And yet, in his own words, he had never once in his life been truly challenged to accept Jesus as his Lord and Saviour. In spite of this, he had attained the most influential lay position in a church with a long and distinguished history. How had he done it? It may seem shocking, but it really shouldn't be. We all know how to play at being Christians, how to say the right things, wear the right clothes, join the right activities, and by doing so avoid uncomfortable questions about our spiritual lives. But looking the part, playing the part, and even fooling everyone else into believing that you are the part is not good enough. It doesn't matter if you are a dead ringer for Billy Graham or if you strongly resemble Johnny Rotten from the Sex Pistols. In the end, it is not our fellow church-goers that we have to convince; they are not the ultimate judges.

- -

THINGS TO DO

Henri Nouwen said this: 'The coming again of Christ is his coming in judgement. The question that will sound through the heavens and the earth will be the question that we always tend to remain deaf to. Our lives as we live them seem like lives that anticipate questions that will never be asked. It seems as if we are getting ourselves ready for the question 'How much did you earn during your lifetime?' or 'How many friends did you make?' or 'How much influence did you have on people?' or 'How many books did you write?' or 'How many conversions did you make?' Were any of these to be the question Christ will ask when he comes again in glory; many of us... could approach the judgement day with great confidence.[9]
Which question dominates your life? What is the question that Jesus will ask when it is time for him to render judgement (Mt. 25)? Do you approach the judgement day with great confidence?

- -

6.3 Future Perfect

LOCATION: 'Have you understood all these things?' Jesus asked. 'Yes,' they replied. He said to them, 'Therefore every teacher of the law who has been instructed about the kingdom of heaven is like the owner of a house

> who brings out of his storeroom new treasures as well as
> old' (Mt. 13:51-52).

I recently heard of a minister who felt he should instruct God to 'Hurry up!' I was horrified by the suggestion that some tin-pot priest would have the nerve to suggest that God was holding everybody back and slowing the revival down. I then began to think over the many times that I have prayed the words of the Lord's Prayer in a similar vein: 'Your kingdom come, your will be done, on earth as it is in heaven.' How many times have I read that as my plea for God to come and do what he hasn't done yet? How often has this prayer offered a devout cover to a very base instinct? 'My kingdom come, my will be done and if you could get a move on I'd much appreciate it, thank you very much.' As Farrar Capon suggests, 'sometimes our prayer hides a thinly veiled attempt to blame our problems on what we think God hasn't done when the truth is we are too lazy to search and find it.[10]

This type of prayer betrays a failure on our part to understand the things Jesus was trying to tell us through the parables. Again, the question ringing through all of these parables is this: 'Do you understand the kingdom?' (Mt. 13:18-23, 51). When Jesus asks his disciples if they understand him, they respond with a 'yes', but we're not sure how confident they are in their answer. We know, in fact, that the disciples miss quite a bit of what Jesus is trying to convey to them. This is evident from their actions during Jesus' arrest and execution. They only really 'get it' after they come face to face with the risen Lord. Things start clicking in their minds. Pennies begin dropping all over the place. 'Oh!' they gasp, 'That's what he was on about! It's him! He's the one! He's the King!' They finally understand that with Jesus, the kingdom has come. With the cross and the resurrection, the kingdom has won.

So now they can truly and honestly bring out of their storerooms treasures both old and new (Mt. 13:52). They can look to Jewish history and the Torah to see how God has shown himself and kept his promises throughout the preceding millennia. Then they can look to Jesus and see how God has revealed himself and is continuing to reveal himself through his Messiah. They can see the treasure of the kingdom of God manifesting itself through history, in the present and into the promised future.

As disciples we too must ask ourselves the question: do we understand the kingdom? The answer is probably not that different from that of the original twelve. We say both 'yes' and 'no.' As you come to the end of this book, do not be disappointed if you feel that the kingdom is still beyond you. It is. The seeking of the kingdom is as important as the finding. Jesus did not instruct his disciples to find the kingdom. Such an expectation would have been beyond the realms of all reality. Jesus called his disciples to seek the kingdom and to seek it before all else.

For any disciple the seeking is as important as the finding, maybe more so. The adventure of the search is all part of the final find. The danger of the journey is part of the joy of the destination. When Ulysses left home he had no idea that his journey would become an Odyssey. The trials and tribulations of his tour with all its victories and failures, successes and disappointments, enriched Homer's hero beyond anything he thought possible. He returned as a hero not because he made it to his destination but because of what happened along the way. So too with kingdom travellers. As you seek the kingdom be ready for all that the King would teach you as a direct result of your search. And don't be afraid to wait for the kingdom. In the kingdom we have the promise of the future in our presence and the hope of glory in our hearts. For the children of the kingdom waiting is hoping and hoping is waiting. The two can never be separated.

Gregory Boyd has suggested that the Lord's Prayer is the perfect example of this mixture of hoping and waiting.[11] It is a celebration of what God has done, is doing and will do with his kingdom. In support of this, Boyd points out that the phrase 'give us today our daily bread' can just as easily be translated as 'give us tomorrow's bread today'. In this prayer we rejoice in the fact that today God has given us a taste of tomorrow. We are not hedonists who know the meaning of nothing except the present moment. We are not like the sage with his monotone mantra: 'Vanity, vanity: everything is vanity.' We are not like the Greek and Roman philosophers of Jesus' day who believed that history was a permanent cycle of events always to be repeated and never to be escaped. History is not the needle returning to the start of the song so we can all sing along like before.

We are the people of the kingdom: the ones who know that the history we see is a front for a much bigger heist. We are the people who know the secrets of creation and the future of the planet. We are the people who are constantly finding the kingdom afresh. We are the people who have discovered that the kingdom is always in us, manifesting its destiny through our little lives. What's more, every time we glimpse or grasp the kingdom, whether in a story, an event, a life or a prayer, we realise that we have been given a bit of forever. We have become part of the purpose of it all and the purpose of it all has become part of us.

If we, as Christ's disciples, have truly discovered and gained some understanding of the kingdom, then God's perfect future is as sure and certain as our imperfect past. We know that the future is not in doubt, just as the present and the past are not in doubt. The King reigns and we, the children of the kingdom, are with him. We are mere subjects living in complete obedience to the King's will and wishes, but we are also royal temples, being made over into glorious dwelling-places for the kingdom and its Sovereign. As we go from place to place and desperately try to live in line with what God has done and God will do, the world sees the kingdom in action, it sees the coming of the King. It sees it in our community and communion with God and with each other; in our worship and service for the King and his kingdom; in our daily duties of work and ministry. In all this we show that there is another way to live, a better day to come, a day when the kingdom will be obvious to everyone and everything. We scream out with our lives that the King is already here and that we are all his subjects; subject to his plans and decrees, whether we recognise it or not. The true sons and daughters of the kingdom have seen tomorrow, today. More than this, they have turned God's plan into their path and God's future into their present.

They have been futurized.

NOTES FROM FELLOW TRAVELLERS

'I think that the books I really enjoy are the ones in which the characters realise, only in the end, what it was that they secretly wanted all along, but never even knew. And maybe this is what life is really like.'

Douglas Coupland[12]

'The mixture of old and new is what Jesus does so well, and teaches us to do. The gospel does not specialise in either ancient history or modern problems, but rather develops the skills to appropriate diverse treasures of the kingdom for redemption goals.'

Eugene Peterson[13]

'Near my flat is the Spanish Consulate. Frequently there are long queues outside – people wanting visas, etc. From time to time a notice appears at the door: "Por favor. Espere acquie." "Please wait here." But it so happens that in Spanish the word espere (wait) is also the word for hope.'

Brian Horne[14]

THINGS TO DO

St Augustine once said:
'Without God, we cannot,
Without us, he will not.'[15]
Spend some time praising God for who he is: the Creator, Governor and Preserver of all things, the Great King of the Universe, and of our lives. Then thank God that he has chosen to place his kingdom in our lives, so we could carry it wherever we go, in order that others might be drawn to become citizens of the Celestial City.

KINGDOM SIGHTINGS

We can catch tantalising glimpses of the kingdom of God in the oddest places. Douglas Coupland, the man who coined the term 'Generation X' wrote a book called *Life After God*. He points out that his is the first generation to grow up without a real mass belief in a god of some sort, and so he analyses in his narrative what life is like *post-deus*. And then, almost bizarrely, we find the following conclusion to his book:

'I peel my clothes and step into the pool beside the burbling stream, onto polished rocks, and the water so clear that it seems it might not even be really there.

My skin is grey, from lack of sun, from lack of bathing. And yes, the water is so cold, this water that only yesterday was locked as ice on the mountaintops. But the pain from the cold is a pain that does not matter to me. I strip my pants, my shirt, my tie, my underwear and they lie strewn on the gravel bar next to my blanket.

And the water from the stream above me roars.

Oh does it roar! Like a voice that knows only one message, one truth – never-ending, like the clapping of hands and the cheers of the citizens upon the coronation of the king, the crowds of the inauguration, cheering for hope and for that one voice that will speak to them.

Now – here is my secret:

I tell it to you with an openness of heart that I doubt I shall ever achieve again, so I pray that you are in a quiet room as you hear these words. My secret is that I need God – that I am sick and can no longer make it alone. I need God to help me give, because I no longer seem to be capable of giving; to help me be kind, as I no longer seem capable of kindness; to help me love, as I seem beyond being able to love.

I walk deeper and deeper into the rushing water....The water enters my belly button and it freezes my chest, my arms, my neck. It reaches my mouth, my nose, my ears and the roar is so loud – this roar, this clapping of hands.

These hands – the hands that heal; the hands that hold; the hands we desire because they are better than desire.

I submerge myself in the pool completely. I grab my knees and I forget gravity and I float within the pool and yet, even here, I hear the roar of water, the roar of clapping hands.

These hands – the hands that care, the hands that mould; the hands that touch the lips, the lips that speak the words – the words that tell us we are whole.'

Douglas Coupland[16]

Is Douglas Coupland living 'life after God' after all? The kingdom is past, present and future. There is no 'after God.'

- -

TOUR GUIDE

'Here is a Torah-teacher who says in his own name what the Torah says in God's name... For what kind of Torah is it that improves upon the teachings of the Torah without acknowledging the source – and it is God who is the source – of those teachings? I am troubled not so much by the message... as I am by the messenger... Sages... say things in their own names, but without claiming to improve upon the Torah. The prophet Moses speaks not in his own name but in God's name, saying what God told him to say. Jesus speaks not as a sage nor as a prophet... So we find ourselves... with the difficulty of making sense, within the framework of the Torah, of a teacher who stands apart from, perhaps above, the Torah... We now recognise that at issue is the figure of Jesus, not the teachings at all.'

Neusner[17]

- -

FINAL PLACE TO STAY

'For all things which seem to make for peace and happiness are nothing, if You are not there, and in truth confer no happiness. For You are the fountain of all good, the height of life, and the depth of all fine speech, and in You above all things to hope, is Your servant's strongest consolation. On You are my eyes, in You I trust, my God, Father of mercies. Bless and sanctify my soul with heavenly blessing, that it may become Your sacred dwelling place, the seat of your eternal glory and that nothing may be found in the temple of Your divinity which could offend the eyes of Your majesty. According to the greatness of Your goodness, and the multitude of Your mercies, look upon me and hear the prayers of Your poor servant, a far exile in the kingdom of the shadow of death. Protect and preserve the soul of Your poor servant amid the many perils of a corruptible life, and, Your grace accompanying, direct him along the path of peace to the fatherland of everlasting light.'

Thomas á Kempis [18]

---

[1] R. H. Gundry, *Matthew: a commentary on his handbook for a mixed church under persecution* (Grand Rapids: W. B. Eerdmans Publishing Co., 1994) p279

[2] J. Bunyan, *The Pilgrim's progress*, edited by N. H. Keeble (Oxford: Oxford University Press, 1998) p11

[3] Jean Vanier, quoted in *A blessed weakness: the spirit of Jean Vanier and l'Arche* (San Francisco: Harper and Row, 1986) p90

[4] Calvin Miller, *The Singer* (Illinois: InterVarsityPress, 1975)

[5] John Newton, published in *The Songbook of the Salvation Army* (London: Salvation Army publishing and supplies, 1986) song 82

[6] T. F. Torrance, *Kingdom and the Church: a study in the theology of the Reformation* (Eugene: Wipf and Stock Publishers, 1996) p15

[7] E. Peterson, *Praying with Jesus* (San Francisco: Harper 1993)

[8] Source unknown

[9] Henri Nouwen, *Seeds of hope: a Henri Nouwen reader* edited Robert Durback (Toronto: Bantam Books 1989) p180

[10] R. F. Capon, *The parables of the kingdom* (Grand Rapids: W. B. Eerdmans Publishing Co., 1985) p45

[11] Gregory Boyd, *God at war: the Bible and spiritual conflict* (Illinois: InterVarsityPress, 1997) p218

[12] Douglas Coupland, *Life after God* (Toronto: Pocket Books, 1994)

[13] E. Peterson, *Praying with Jesus* (San Francisco: Harper, 1993)

[14] Source unknown

[15] St. Augustine, quoted in Richard Foster's *Streams of living water: celebrating the great traditions of the Christian faith* (San Francisco: Harper San Francisco, 1998) p197

[16] Douglas Coupland, *Life after God* (Toronto: Pocket Books, 1994)

[17] Neusner, quoted in N. T. Wright, *Jesus and the victory of God* (London: SPCK, 1996) p646

[18] Thomas á Kempis, *The imitation of Christ* (London: Blackie and Son, 1920)